QUAKE CHASERS

15
WOMEN ROCKING EARTHQUAKE SCIENCE

LORI POLYDOROS

Copyright © 2022 by Lori Polydoros

All rights reserved

Published by Chicago Review Press Incorporated

814 North Franklin Street

Chicago, Illinois 60610

ISBN 978-1-64160-646-2

Library of Congress Control Number: 2021949118

Cover, illustrations, and interior design: Sadie Teper

Printed in the United States of America

5 4 3 2 1

To all the future scientists . . . the best is yet to come.

Contents

Introduction

Sometimes, the world needs saving. When nature wreaks havoc with earthquakes, tsunamis, and erupting volcanoes, we want a superhero to fly out of the sky save the day.

But what if these "superheroes" lived and worked among us? What if, instead of flying and superstrength, these world savers use laboratories and laptops? These brave women are earthquake scientists who venture into the field and experiment in labs. They use advanced technology to translate data on their laptops gathered from postdisaster recovery sites to find out what caused that earthquake, triggered that tsunami, or led that volcano to erupt. These "quake chasers" can be found scrambling to install seismometers on erupting volcanoes, arctic glaciers, or deep in the sunbaked desert. They measure ground motion, observe geological structures of the earth, tell the stories of survivors, and communicate vital data to the public that helps people prepare for potential seismic events. These women help save lives.

Donyelle Davis, a public affairs officer from both the US Geological Survey and the US Navy Reserve, is afraid of heights yet needed to get information about the eruption of Hawaii's Kīlauea volcano out to the public. With eyes closed (only at first), she put her fears aside and, in a tiny aircraft, flew over the bubbling lava to record images of the destruction. Or take geophysicist Dr. Marianne Karplus, who journeyed to Nepal after a magnitude 7.8 quake killed almost 9,000 people. In order to record vital information about aftershocks, she placed seismometers across the rupture zone. While she was working, the ground shook with aftershocks, creating cracks in the walls, but she didn't stop working. Another quake chaser is geologist Dr. Wendy Bohon, who you might find deep in a trench carefully reading the earth's history through rocks or mapping massive, inaccessible peaks in South America with satellite technology, all to gather data along fault lines that could reveal important facts about future earthquakes. This information can help people prepare and stay safe.

These women are trailblazers. They are seismologists, geophysicists, geologists, physicists, volcanologists, professors, social scientists, and communication specialists. They come from different specialties, yet their commonalities tie them together: Strength. Curiosity. Persistence. They never give up, even when a door closes. Nor are they afraid to call out gender or racial injustice when they see it—and unfortunately for women in STEM (science, technology, engineering, mathematics) fields, these inequities can be common.

Many of these scientists know each other, whether working together in the field or collaborating on projects worldwide. They respect each other. Rely on each other. They've become mentors and have found their own inspiration and strength through other women in the field. Traveling the world with a special lens for saving lives, most have carefully crafted a deep respect for cultures, languages, and interesting food (plus karaoke it seems!). Through science-related and fictional books and industry journals and newsletters, many communicate their messages and share their camaraderie for humanizing science, opening doors for other women, and inspiring others to chase their dreams.

Quake Chasers focuses on just 15 of these amazing women. There are so many more incredible women in earthquake science, in all fields of science, and in every aspect of our world. We are just waiting to meet them!

So for now, let's hear it for the quake chasers!

Fifteen women who rock earthquake science.

Part I
SOS: The Secrets of Seismic Hazards

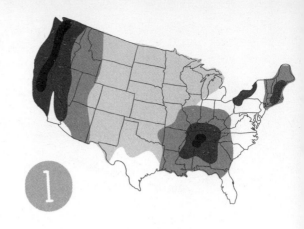

Annemarie Baltay Sundstrom: The Power of Predicting

Award-winning geophysicist Dr. Annemarie Baltay Sundstrom spends her days measuring the ground motion of the earth. Yet you might find her doing some unusual things, like singing karaoke in Japan and belting out the 1980s pop hit "99 Red Balloons" in German! Whether skiing down a scary mountain ridge or analyzing data to better understand earthquakes, Annemarie has pushed herself further than she ever imagined. Her curiosity and confidence, encouraged by her scientific parents, have taken Annemarie down a road of discovery. From an early age she's been who she's wanted to be and hasn't been afraid to speak her mind. Whether doing experiments in the garden with her mother or making furniture in her father's woodshop, Annemarie was given the chance to follow her dreams.

As a seismologist with the US Geological Survey, Annemarie asks questions like: Why do some earthquakes behave differently? How do earth materials change the (recorded) ground motion/shaking? Using this data, Annemarie creates hazard maps that show earthquake danger zones and help warn people about possible disasters in the future. At her computer, Annemarie analyzes data from big events like the magnitude (M) 9.1 earthquake and the tsunami that followed in Sumatra in 2004. This earthquake, which killed 230,000 people, was the third largest in the world since 1900. She also has analyzed the magnitude 9.1 quake in Japan in 2011. It trigged a tsunami with waves as tall as a 38-story building, flooding more than 200 square miles of land and leaving approximately 20,000 people dead or missing and half a million without homes. Though these events are tragic, Annemarie knows her work can make a difference. Walking this path has not always been easy, but Annemarie is grateful for all the support and opportunities she has received, even when facing her own doubt and uncertainty. For her, it's all worth it. It's always been about uncovering the mysteries below the earth and using this information to save lives.

Annemarie's parents told her that she could be whatever she wanted, and for that she is forever grateful. Her father, a particle physicist who worked at Yale University (and collaborated with other scientists at Stanford University), and her mother, a seventh-grade science teacher and college writing instructor, encouraged her to follow her own path and to "do something important." Annemarie had a lot of freedom and remembers happy summers at Stanford with her mother, picking berries, drawing, building, or doing backyard experiments, like mixing gross ingredients such as vanilla and vinegar and making her mom drink it! In Connecticut, she grew up by the water, where she learned to swim and sail. In the marsh nearby, she played tag in the mucky trails and looked for frogs and snails all day long. Annemarie's dad gave her notebooks full of math problems for long car rides and allowed her to use his woodshop, where she built furniture (for people and for her toy figurines) and learned to solder and work with metal too.

From physics to lacrosse, Annemarie didn't just belong to one friend group in high school. Motivated by the adrenaline and determination of running sports like lacrosse, she became cocaptain of the team senior year. She found a home on the physics team too—thriving on the intellectual challenge and her teammates' enthusiasm for science (even after Annemarie's heartbreak of not making the team junior year).

At times, though, gender stereotypes in math and science were visible. While earning the math award on Senior Night, her father overhead someone say, "She's too pretty to be a mathematician." Annmarie's parents taught her that all people should have the opportunity to work toward their dreams, regardless of old-fashioned social and gender norms. She was lucky to have such big supporters in her parents, who always stood up for her and believed the sky was the limit for their daughter. And, that it was. Yet she acknowledges that gender bias against women in math and science is real and believes society must fight against the limits or norms put on boys and girls—whether for play or in school. Annemarie believes that "boys should be allowed to play with dolls and girls allowed to play with trucks." She also believes that math and science should not be gender specific. Kids are super curious, she believes, and want to learn numbers and logic—and both boys and girls should definitely be encouraged to do so. As a parent herself, Annemarie believes in being open-minded and encourages her kids to do well at whatever they put their mind to—especially if it involves cool subjects like physics, chemistry, math, and statistics—which she says is a must for *everyone.*

In Search of an Even Playing Field

Over time, expectations for both girls and boys have changed, and many social scientists today know that all children need the chance to explore different gender roles and styles of play. Today, female athletes are given the opportunity to excel at sports, but that was not always the case. Gender bias and stereotypes can be found as far back as ancient Greece. The modern Olympics emerged in the late nineteenth century, but female athletes were not allowed to compete. During the 1920s and '30s, the Women's Olympic Games provided women the chance to display their skills. However, women who pushed against social norms and played sports were often negatively labeled as "rough girls." Due to sexism, along with other issues such as racial segregation, female athletes continued to be excluded from professional sports. But when World War II struck and the country needed strong women to enter the workforce, norms changed. It was during this time that "Rosie the Riveter," a symbolic female figure that represented female factory and shipyard workers, and the All-American Girls Professional Baseball League appeared.

Yet for the next three decades, racial segregation and gender exclusion still dictated US sports heroes and left behind many athletic hopefuls. Finally, by the early 1970s, in the wake of the civil rights and feminist movements, women and athletes of underrepresented groups found a place on the field, court, track, or pool. In 1972 Title IX became law, making it illegal to exclude any American from participating in athletics due to gender.

But the road to equality and fairness in sports had just begun. Through the twentieth and into the twenty-first century, women are still fighting for equal rights and fair pay in all levels of sports. Advocates will continue to break barriers and change the rules until everyone can finally run, swim, kick, throw, and shoot on an even playing field.

After studying geophysics at Yale, Annemarie's father encouraged her to get a postdoctoral degree (PhD) instead of becoming a middle school science teacher like she had planned. Her dad "was always right," and things just fell into place. Annemarie received a full scholarship for her PhD degree in geophysics at Stanford. Even though she loved science, she didn't dream about it all day and just couldn't see herself as a professor. She kept asking herself, *What am I going to do with my life?* Both her PhD mentor, Greg Beroza, and her postdoc mentor, Tom Hanks (not the actor), were incredibly supportive. Both became her "intellectual cheerleaders," walking the fine line between backing her up and pushing her into the spotlight.

Annemarie acknowledges the imposter syndrome she felt—not feeling good enough, smart enough, or not knowing if she was cut out to do research. But then she realized that everyone else felt the same way. In grad school, she was looking for affirmation and felt like she was surrounded by people who had it all figured out. Slowly, she began to build her confidence by leading discussions and taking leadership roles. With time and experience, Annemarie began to feel validated and realized that everyone was on the same playing field. She says it's like watching ducks in a pond, and if you "look underwater, [you'll] see everyone is paddling and you are not alone."

Travel is one aspect Annemarie loves about her field. On a summer internship in Japan, she became an expert at karaoke and met colleagues from all over the world. Annemarie grew to appreciate the connection she had with her Japanese collaborators. As a scientist, she knows the importance of critical thinking and multiple perspectives, acknowledging the awareness that experiencing other cultures brings about: "If you can imagine a second language, you can imagine 27 more." She did notice that gender norms at conferences in Japan were "much more strict . . . and there were no women scientists, only secretaries dressed in black suits." Even though she believes this inequity is slowly improving, Annemarie's observations seem to hold true. The Japanese Cabinet Office's 2017 report on gender equality stated that throughout all fields, including in the social sciences, only 15.3 percent of Japanese researchers were women.

As a scientist (and human being), Annemarie feels it is vital to understand the cultures of others and connect through our similarities—to understand that we are all human and the same things are important to everyone. She is hopeful that the changes in access and expectations for women in science will improve globally.

The Global Glass Ceiling

In Japan, the bias against women in STEM has a name—*rikejo*, which translates to a negative way to say "science women." Culturally, many parents and teachers believe that if a girl follows a path into science or math, it will hurt her chances at getting a job or in relationships with men. Men in high positions in the scientific field worry that hiring a woman will put their teams at a disadvantage for funding or getting their research published (though some research shows that female researchers produced more scholarly papers than their male counterparts between 2011 and 2015). This discrimination also reinforces the idea that women should focus on home and family—a cultural norm in many countries around the world, as UNESCO (the United Nations Educational, Scientific, and Cultural Organization) reports that just 30 percent of the world's researchers are women.

Annemarie appreciates that in the United States the system is moving toward more equality for women in STEM fields, but the road still has its bumps. In her postdoctoral program, there were few women mentors, and due to this gender gap, male advisors often still held the only seats at the table. But she never felt like she couldn't speak her mind and is grateful for all her supportive advisers, male and female. As she grew into this confidence, Annemarie's research grew in strides as well, bridging a new gap that connected the work of seismologists and engineers. She used this data to think about how and when earthquakes might happen. By carving out a new way of studying earthquakes, Annemarie was nominated for and received the prestigious Charles F. Richter Early Career Award at a young age. She had already begun to make her mark!

As a research geophysicist at the US Geological Survey (USGS), Annemarie works alongside many incredible female scientists and has found her support system. Her main focus is to improve communications between seismologists and engineers in hopes of improving ground motion models that connect a quake to the possible shaking that might happen, and hazard maps, information that can prevent damage and loss of life during a quake. She wants people to understand how a distant earthquake can affect the shaking at their own home.

Through previous earthquake data from magnitude (size) and distance, Annemarie asks questions and looks for trends and new interpretations. Currently, in California, these models assume that motion travels similarly across all kinds of terrain. Using physics, Annemarie wants to create more accurate models and understand what properties and materials make the ground shake more or less fiercely. Previously, these models were only based on recordings of past earthquakes, but her research combines statistical observations with the physics of the earth, such as rocks, properties, structures, and heat flow.

Annemarie's team also analyzes the topography, or the arrangement of the natural and physical features of an area, to gain insight into predicting these effects. In addition, she works to develop the best ways to model ground motion in early warning systems, like the USGS ShakeAlert, an early warning project that aims to alert the West Coast before an earthquake strikes.

West Coast ShakeAlert System

Today, in California, Oregon, and Washington, the USGS ShakeAlert Earthquake Early Warning System detects substantial quakes and sends a real-time alert to mobile devices through text-like messaging, displaying warnings such as: EARTHQUAKE DETECTED! DROP, COVER, HOLD ON. PROTECT YOURSELF. ShakeAlert technology cannot predict the location or date of an earthquake, but it can identify a quake that has already begun, giving people advance warning that allows them a few seconds to perform lifesaving measures, like taking personal protective action and turning off water and utility valves. This technology will prevent damage and loss of life and is available to all mobile phones that have Wireless Emergency Alerts (WEA) turned on or through various apps.

As a geophysicist, Annemarie's daily life involves more than just numbers. The role of writing is huge as it is still the main form of communication in her field. She says that scientific writing is different from other forms of writing, and one needs to be able to convey their research concisely and clearly. Yet writing hasn't always come easy to her. She remembers her mom helping her in high school on late-night writing sessions the night before a paper was due. Annemarie has had to work at perfecting her craft, even though she's struggled with writing most of her life.

As a part of her duties, Annemarie publishes scientific papers every year and must write reports, updates, and summaries. She also has to justify the need for postdocs and funding, proving how it all moves her science forward. She gathers digital data recorded at seismic stations globally and downloads this information straight to her computer, where she uses MATLAP programming language to process the data, make plots, and pull out trends. From there, she writes her paper, collaborates with her colleagues, and reviews other people's work. The work never stops. But neither will Annmarie's passion for figuring out how to save people from the shaking under the earth.

There is so much Annemarie loves about her job. She says, "I was brought up to respect that science is important, and I believe that." Her field is based on logic, and she finds solace in determining how she can solve problems. She enjoys working with others who value these same things.

Annemarie often visits classrooms, gives presentations, and interacts with the public. She gets especially excited when people show enthusiasm about her research. She can see how she's contributing to the greater understanding of how to save people's lives during a big quake. For her, it's even more personal though. After completing a master's degree in English at UMass Amherst, her mother became pregnant with one of Annemarie's brothers. Her mother had been enrolled in a PhD program, but Annemarie's father was already a professor at Columbia, and because of the distance between the two schools (and no remote learning possibilities like today), her mother wasn't able to complete her doctoral program. Annemarie now honors her mother by striving for excellence in this often challenging, yet exhilarating world of earthquake science. Although many people say their mother is their biggest inspiration, Annemarie really means it.

As a young mom of two young boys, Annemarie does it all too. She tries not to be a "helicopter mom" and teaches her kids to be independent thinkers and real people instead of real rule followers. Everyone has their own role in her family, and she and her husband believe in not just equality but also equity at home. She's able to have a good work-family balance, finding time to make her kids' Halloween costumes, to build silly animals out of paper towel tubes, and to spend time in her small woodshop in the garage.

Annemarie is quite adventurous. On their honeymoon in Alaska, she and her husband went heli-skiing—skiing down tall peaks after being dropped off by helicopter. She takes her kids on adventures too, but the last time she took her son skiing, she ended up on a helicopter for a different reason: her son skied into a tree and wound up in the emergency room. She stayed calm but felt horrible for not being able to protect him. They made it through, and after some healing, her son got right back to skiing.

Get back up when you fall down. That's something Annemarie has learned as a student, scientist, and mom. She's grateful for all the opportunities in her life, and especially excited about the ways her research can help improve lives and save people during earthquakes. But Annemarie is just getting started with her innovative research and insight and believes wholeheartedly that "anything is possible."

Annemarie's Top Three Tips for Earthquake Safety

Have a plan with those you live with: What will you do when the shaking hits? How will you communicate? Who will your "check-in" person be if you and your family get separated?

Layer your favorite foods in your emergency kit. How many cans of tuna do you really want to have?

Place a sticker on your home's window that tells how many pets you have—gotta remember our furry friends!

Follow Annemarie Baltay Sundstrom Online:

Website: www.usgs.gov/staff-profiles/annemarie-baltay

Twitter: @USGS_Quakes and @USGS_ShakeAlert

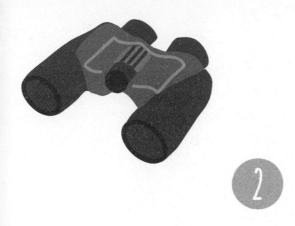

Wendy Bohon:
This Is What a Scientist Looks Like

It's hard to find a more inspirational role model for women in science than Dr. Wendy Bohon, a geologist and science communication specialist for the Incorporated Research Institutions for Seismology (IRIS) in Washington, DC. Wendy grew up on a farm surrounded by nature and quickly fell into the arts—acting, writing, and poetry. But taking her first geology class in college allowed her to fully embrace the love she has for the inner workings of the earth.

Wendy is passionate about studying earthquakes and communicating how the science behind them saves lives. She's also a fierce activist, battling systemic issues such as gender bias and racism in the field of science, which promote inequities. She's a volunteer for the nonprofit group 500 Women Scientists, an organization with 20,000 members whose goal is to make science and society safer and more inclusive, fighting against discriminatory social norms, racism, and patriarchy. It's a grassroots organization that fights societal inequities. You might find Wendy at an event proudly wearing her Unapologetically Feminist Scientist T-shirt or see the life-size statue of her as the *#IfThenSheCan* ambassador for the organization's exhibit, which highlights 122 contemporary female STEM professionals. Wherever she goes, Wendy uses her wisdom, experience, and the power she's earned as a scientist to speak up for others and make change in the world.

Wendy wants to know the earth's stories. Often found deep in a trench listening to what the rocks tell us about the past, she has deployed with many field teams around the world. In the Himalayas, she mapped big faults on massive peaks. In hard-to-reach places in the Andes Mountains, she gathered data from faults. She also worked in precarious places on the borders of India, China, and Pakistan. Wendy packs in her enthusiasm and resilience to study the changes in the earth's surface, and no matter which part of the planet she travels to, she approaches her research with compassion and empathy.

Wendy's first career was as an actress, and she has worked hard over the years to develop her own scientific identity. Whether working in a lab, giving a presentation, or even sitting in a trench, Wendy is enthused about all her discoveries. But the path has not been easy, and mistreatment from some men in the field has made her question herself. Yet she's found a network of supportive people who believe in her, and she's learned over the years to recognize her own power and use it to push back. Wendy has found pride in being a mother of three (including rambunctious twin boys), a wife, a scientist, and an activist. It's hard to balance all her roles, but Wendy knows that by living in this beautiful chaos, she can help others see that their passions can be found in many places.

Raised on a family farm in Virginia, Wendy and her sister grew up with their grandma and aunt living as neighbors. In the wheat, corn, and soybean fields, she had nature outside her front door, and without cable TV, there was nothing to do but read, go outside, build forts, and explore. She learned to love books early on, as nobody could read to her enough to satiate her hunger for stories. To this day, she devours everything she can, from fantasy to romance, and especially loves Harry Potter books or anything zombie and apocalypse related!

As an energetic kid, Wendy says she drove her mom nuts with questions. Her father was an optometrist, karate teacher, and naturalist. He kept a real human skeleton in the garage and taught everyone about the bones in the body. Wendy joined him on the excursions he led at the park, and she could identify every shell, tree, and bird in their area. As a Girl Scout, Wendy took caving trips and will never forget lying on a cave floor and staring at a fossilized shell lodged in the cave wall. Seeing a fossil of a seashell 100 miles from the ocean blew Wendy's mind.

Wendy didn't start out in science. As an actress, she performed in Shakespearean plays and wrote poetry too, studying both theater and geology at James Madison University. After taking a geology class in a huge lecture hall of 250 students, Wendy couldn't stop her mind from racing about all things geology, even though many of the other students in the class were bored or asleep. Wendy took more geology classes and believed that geologists, who often brought their dogs to class, were super cool.

In 1999, while pursuing acting in Los Angeles, the magnitude 7.1 Hector Mine earthquake hit (centered in the Mojave Desert), and it forever shook up Wendy's life. The shaking ground invigorated her. She rushed to the US Geological Survey (USGS) office at the California Institute of Technology in Pasadena to volunteer. In the midst of the chaos, Wendy was sent home, but she didn't give up. She returned to the office, where she met Lisa Wald and Dr. Lucy Jones, the "reason she became a scientist," who allowed her to work on a project to demonstrate her knowledge and passion. Hired soon after as the USGS outreach and education specialist, Wendy used her knowledge to teach people how to be less anxious and how to stay safe in scary situations, to help activate the science by turning data into policy and building codes to keep people from harm.

Lucy Jones: The Earthquake Expert

Dr. Lucy Jones, one of the world's most influential seismologists, spent 33 years at the USGS. She has written or cowritten 90 research papers and was one of the first scientists to use statistics to predict that one quake could lead to bigger and more dangerous ones. She's had a presence in the media and is especially remembered for holding her one-year-old son in a TV interview after the 1992 magnitude 6.1 Joshua Tree quake, which made her more relatable and more human, and gave the scientific community a face that could comfort people.

Lucy's childhood revolved around science and math, yet she grew up during a time when girls weren't ushered into these male-centered fields. She followed her own road, studying Chinese literature and physics at Brown University. After taking her first geology class during senior year, she was hooked! As a PhD student in geophysics at the Massachusetts Institute of Technology, Lucy was just one of two women in her program. In 1979, after China opened its doors to Westerners, she became one of the first American scientists to study earthquakes there.

Traveling worldwide to places like Afghanistan, New Zealand, and Japan, Lucy presented research that demonstrates how fault systems can help scientists predict possible future seismic events, like a possible Big One, which some scientists say is overdue in Los Angeles. In order to foresee possible damage and responses, in 2008 Lucy and her team used the ShakeOut scenario to simulate a magnitude 7.8 quake and its consequences. If an earthquake of this magnitude was to strike Los Angeles, they predicted landslides and massive damage, in addition to 2,000 deaths and 50,000 injuries. Today, millions are participating in drills like the ShakeOut, and through her outreach at the Dr. Lucy Jones Center for Science and Society, Lucy continues to bring science to the people so policy makers can activate the information. Lucy will never stop fighting to keep people safe from disaster.

But the road for Wendy was sometimes rocky. Throughout her graduate degree, she faced overt sexism and harassment, and became too familiar with certain men devaluing her science or passing her over for fieldwork. She questioned herself, unsure if this treatment was due to her abilities or gender bias. As a second-year master's student, she attended a conference, where a senior scientist took interest in her work. Later, when he asked her to meet him at a restaurant, she found out that he wasn't at all interested in her research. What hurt even more is when another male student from her program said the misunderstanding was her fault, that she should have seen the red flag and questioned why anyone would be interested in what she had to say. At another conference, after being introduced to colleagues, the men joked and made inappropriate comments that insulted her intelligence and capabilities. Years later, one of the young men apologized for what had happened—but it still stung.

This recurring theme of doubt shadowed her life, and she didn't always feel as if she belonged or was worthy to be in her field. A few years ago, during a meeting, Wendy was fixing her hair when a male colleague asked her to stop because it was distracting the other men. Fortunately, another guy in the room told him to stop. This was the first time in her life that one man had called out a microaggression, or demeaning comment, in front of another.

Wendy does believe that, despite the harassment and discrimination that still exists, women are much less willing to take it now and are in a space where these things can be talked about. By pulling this behavior "into the light," sexism will begin to dwindle. She doesn't believe gender inequities will ever go away completely, but Wendy is hopeful things are getting better. She advises young women to find their tribe at work or school and be that support for others. Believe in your own abilities, Wendy says, and appreciate your uniqueness, your own power, because nobody has the same gifts as you. Wendy encourages people to figure out their own space of power and push back hard. "If we all push in those places, we can move the system."

Wendy has found her place in earthquake science, along with many of the women in this very book, like Dr. Lucy Jones, doctoral student Beth Bartel, and Dr. Sue Hough. With their support, she has been able to embrace her scientific identity and move forward with confidence so she can do the science and save lives.

With this confidence, Wendy makes it a priority to stand up as a role model to other women in science. "We can't have equality for women until we have equality for all," Wendy says. Some people, who didn't appreciate women taking up certain space, pushed back against this message. As 500 Women Scientists' global communication representative for four years, Wendy even got death threats. As a part of the *#IfThenSheCan* exhibit taking place in fall 2021 in Dallas, Texas, Wendy's life-size 3-D-printed image will stand proudly alongside the images of 121 other female scientists, normalizing women in power and giving them the acclaim they deserve.

The Smithsonian reports that out of the more than 5,000 statues depicting historical figures in the United States, only about 400 of them are of women. This lack of representation demonstrates how women have been cut out of the narrative of our collective stories, taking away the role they've played in our country, especially in STEM-related fields. The *#IfThenSheCan* exhibit will be the largest collection of images of women. With the 3-D data available, Wendy has even been able to make action figures and Christmas ornaments for her family.

Scientist Barbies

Imagine a Barbie doll that comes with hiking boots and a magnifying glass instead of pearls and a fancy dress. It's taken years for female scientists to find their place in the world, and now Nalini Nadkarni, a forest ecologist who studies rainforest canopies, has helped Mattel and National Geographic design a line of dolls to represent just that. There's an astrophysicist, conservationist, entomologist, marine biologist, and a nature photojournalist.

"These explorer Barbies are a big step forward," Nalini said, still a bit weary of their unrealistic body type. "It's not perfect . . . but it's a good start." She never played with Barbies as a girl. Instead, Nalini loved climbing trees, and today she's a biology professor at the University of Utah.

It's about time women in STEM get representation in the world of play. The only thing missing? An earthquake scientist!

In the field, Wendy uses many geological methods to figure out Earth's past, such as remote sensing or geological mapping.

In order to reveal a rock's time clock, researchers also use processes to determine how long a rock has been exposed at the surface and how certain rocks moved through the crust. With this information, Wendy can almost rewind time and get a glimpse of natural events of the past so she can better predict future seismic activity. Some might say she's that crazy scientist who sits inside a dirt trench and stares at the walls, but she loves it!

Once she starts mapping the earth, the rocks start to tell their story and Wendy says it's an exploration, like reading a good book. By examining the horizontal layer of rock, geologists look for breaks, bends, or changes. They can picture if the land was once a desert or a bog, or if the wind was blowing, or if a rodent had dug a burrow there.

When the data works, Wendy says it's mind-blowing to generate new knowledge. But scientists must check their work a thousand times to make sure it's right; there is no answer key. And even if the science doesn't work, it's still exciting when you're wrong and you find something you didn't expect. Mapping out an entire fault can allow researchers to predict how big the quake might be, as magnitude is based on how long of a section of the fault ruptures.

Reading the Rock Clock

As a geologist, Wendy uses different methods, such as cosmogenic nuclide dating (CRN) or noble gas geochronology, in order to reveal a rock's past. To estimate the age of a rock, CRN uses the interaction between cosmic rays (high-energy particles that flow into our solar system from outer space) and nuclides (a certain kind of atom or nucleus associated with a specific number of protons and neutrons). Through this process, scientists can tell how long a rock has been on the surface, which gives them a better indication of the time period.

Through noble gas geochronology, researchers study when a rock's clock starts and minerals from deep in the earth begin to move toward the surface. These minerals contain radioactive elements that create gasses like helium, which may come and go until the rock cools. At that point, Wendy says, "a door shuts" and geologists can use the composition to determine how the rock moved through the crust toward the surface, thus figuring out its age and more about the earth's earthquake history.

Throughout her education and career, Wendy has asked many questions about big earthquake faults worldwide. In South America, Wendy mapped areas in Argentina that showed an increase in faults along what she calls "the baby mountain nursery" in the Andes Mountains, gathering data about how specific faults have changed over time. Her data revealed that the fault system didn't reach the surface (called a blind thrust fault) and had started slipping more quickly over the last 3,000 years. Wendy's team realized that this information increased the possibility of a future earthquake, giving the area more of a hazard potential.

In the Himalayas in India, Wendy focused on a massive fault similar to the San Andreas fault of California. Little is known about the fault, and large parts have never been reached. But working in hard-to-access terrain and dealing with countries in political conflict made gathering data along this partially unmapped fault challenging. With peaks as high as K2 nearby (more than 28,000 feet), Wendy and her team tried something only done to study outer space. Working from the Mars Spaceflight Facility at Arizona State University, they used remote satellites to take pictures, or space maps, of the mineral composition of the ground in the isolated peaks, revealing how this fault may have changed over time.

On the border of India, China, and Pakistan, Wendy's team had to cross many fences, walls, and military bases (and return every 8 to10 days to get passports checked), plus work carefully to avoid dangerous areas with unexploded land mines or military troops. By gathering information from long ago, her team discovered how a second strand of one of the faults has been active in the last 10,000 years and a nearby mountain range had evolved over the last 25 million years. They gained insight into how the faults interacted with each other, which can influence potential quakes in the area.

For Wendy, research is not only about science but also about the people—finding the best ways to help them prepare for disaster and stay safe. In the Himalayas, everybody was lovely and warm. Wendy remembers a man with an injured hand walking alongside the road. He had just been in a construction accident. He needed medical attention, and Wendy's team performed what first aid they could, but Wendy says it is so difficult to not be able to help the people who need it.

When it comes to preparing for disasters, Wendy knows that not all people are on an equal playing field. By placing the responsibility on individuals, the system doesn't take into consideration cultural, social, or economic gaps that may prevent those in the most danger from being able to keep their families safe during a quake. Not all families can afford to buy enough food or water for two weeks or to evacuate quickly if they rely on public transportation. It's unfair, Wendy says, to put the total burden of action on the people who will suffer the most and be the least likely to be able to cope. These systemic issues that turn natural events into disasters need to be addressed. We need to start learning from the past, she says, and it's about time to start adjusting to the changes in our world.

People must become educated, and the science that experts gather must be put into place so that new policies and regulations can save all lives, regardless of any societal inequities. Government, faith, and community leaders must have access to the science so that they can convince others to invest in preparation before a natural disaster takes place. Society needs to stop being reactive and start being proactive.

Wendy's role as the science communication specialist for IRIS allows her to work on translating the data. Through storytelling, social media, and networking classes, she teaches scientists to talk more effectively and freely about their science with each other, to policymakers, and to a broader audience. Wendy wants to help give those in charge the tools they need to put science into action.

Wendy loves what she does and has come to understand that the "earth will tell you it's secrets, if you just take the time to listen." By communicating these secrets, she hopes to help officials activate the science so that lives can be saved when a Big One, a hypothetical earthquake of magnitude 8 or more along the San Andreas fault, shakes the ground next. She's grateful that she did not follow a traditional path into science and, more important, proud of carving out her own road.

At home, Wendy's a dedicated wife and a proud mama of three kids plus three furry rescues: cranky old Mr. Cat, crazy kitten Mrs. Norris, and Brody, a crazy pup afraid of the refrigerator and the bathroom. She writes a thoughtful blog called *Twinning at Motherhood* in order to share her stories with other moms of twins, and she is working on writing a memoir as well.

Among all of Wendy's passions, you can find one common theme: she wants to fix what's broken so that others don't have to go through avoidable struggles. Wendy wants to change the system and protect people so that life can be full of joy and not sadness.

Wendy's Top Three Tips for Earthquake Safety

Don't forget to have extra food and water for your pets in your emergency kit—they're part of the family too!

Make sure to have extra medications on hand. Supply lines can be delayed after large earthquakes.

Keep shoes next to your bed. Many things can fall and break during earthquakes, and shoes will protect your feet.

Follow Wendy Bohon Online:

Website: https://drwendybohon.com/

Instagram: @DrWendyRocks

Twitter: @DrWendyRocks

Facebook: www.facebook.com/DrWendyRocks

YouTube: www.youtube.com/channel/UCattuUO9_ytbURJ
IOJahlg

Peggy Hellweg: The Explainer

As one of seven children raised by physicist parents, Dr. Peggy Hellweg started asking questions about how the world worked at a very young age. Whether solving puzzles or staring at the sky with her father, Peggy learned quickly that these questions could be solved through science. She used her critical thinking skills to succeed in tough situations, like moving to Austria when she was eight, or working as a "walking encyclopedia" as a teenager at the famous Exploratorium science museum.

Throughout her career, Peggy has studied strong motion earthquakes and even data from bubbling volcanoes. As the operations manager for the Berkeley Seismological Laboratory in California, she has worked hard and collaborated with many organizations in hopes of making early warning systems available to people worldwide. Peggy loves talking about what she's learned and wants to share her knowledge as much as possible.

She has a close connection to nature and likes to mentor and teach this natural bond to kids. Fiercely dedicated to her family, Peggy spreads her love of science and reading to her own children, her grandchildren, and even her many nieces and nephews who soak up all the knowledge and enthusiasm this cool grandma and aunt has to offer.

Above all, Peggy believes in being prepared and teaching others to do the same. She hopes to save as many lives as possible when the Big One hits. And she will continue to explain what's happening under the earth and how we can stay safe and save lives when the ground starts to shake under our feet.

As far back as she can remember, Peggy longed to figure out the answers to the mysteries around her. At a very young age, she remembers wondering why the sky above was blue. (She thought it was the inside of God's belly.) As she grew, her questions grew too. Peggy's mother and father developed a science curriculum study and practiced theories on their own kids. It seemed that a day didn't go by that Peggy didn't think about *thinking*, constantly curious about everything. On a family camping trip in Northern California, Peggy and her father sat atop their car on a bluff and watched a total lunar eclipse. Peggy explained to her father that a total lunar eclipse is when the earth moves in between the sun and the full moon, the earth's shadow covering the moon. Her father always respected and validated what she had to say.

Peggy has loved animals her whole life. As a child, she had two goldfish, a turtle, and several mice that escaped into the basement and made nests. Peggy caught quick-moving lizards, skinks, and frogs, and she still does today, although she's not as fast as she used to be. One time, she even got bit by a garter snake . . . and didn't tell her parents that she was somewhere she shouldn't have been. Peggy can't remember a time when she was not trying to figure out how nature and science worked: eclipses, long division and multiplication tables, car engines. This future physicist never stopped asking *why*.

As second oldest, Peggy didn't like her brothers and sisters telling her what to do. Her first leadership role was as the organizer in the family. When her family moved to Austria, Peggy had to find a way to learn the local language, German. One day at school, each student had to stand up and answer a multiplication problem in front of the class and Peggy hadn't yet learned her times tables. This didn't faze her, though, and Peggy did her best to answer the question in German (even though she thinks she got the answer wrong). New school. New language. New country. Peggy never gave up. She held her head high as she walked to school with her siblings. The kids stuck together. Learned together. Played together. Living in Austria wasn't always easy, but it taught Peggy that people are people, even if they think and do things differently.

All kinds of languages, cultures, and perspectives make life more interesting, and when traveling, Peggy is curious and appreciates the diversity of how people in different cultures and geographical locations live. When she traveled to Russia and China, she learned new words in both languages. While in China, many of Peggy's hosts were hesitant to use English because they felt they would make mistakes, yet Peggy tried to speak Chinese, even though she mispronounced just about everything. In every new place, Peggy wants to understand what people are saying, how they do things, and why they do what they do. In China, she showed everybody she wasn't afraid to try, and that inspired others. After witnessing Peggy's courage, her hosts weren't embarrassed to use their English anymore.

The Exploratorium

As a part of the Manhattan Project in Los Alamos, New Mexico, during World War II, physicist Frank Oppenheimer (along with his brother Robert Oppenheimer) joined the top-secret effort to create an atomic bomb. After the war, the US government forced Frank to resign from his job as a professor at the University of Minnesota for being associated with the American Communist party during the anti-Communist drive following World War II.

Frank was blacklisted, or prevented from getting any other jobs teaching physics, and went from nuclear physicist to cattle rancher. Eventually, in 1957, he was able to return to teaching at the high school level and, later, college science.

After exploring Europe on a Guggenheim Fellowship in 1965, he wanted to create a science museum that would support science taught in US schools. In 1969 Frank opened the Exploratorium in San Francisco, finding new ways of looking at things and promoting a respect for innovation and play.

Today hundreds of thousands of people visit this learning laboratory and playground per year, with 24 million on average visiting its website. The museum houses more than 650 exhibits that center around science, art, and human perception, and is dedicated to experimentation, discovery, tinkering, and play.

As the first "explainer" at the famous Exploratorium in San Francisco, Peggy acted as living encyclopedia for visitors, and enjoyed talking with people and helping them see the wonderful and exciting world they lived in. As one of the first exhibits, the museum displayed a demonstration of the Stanford linear accelerator, which hurls electrons in a straight line. This accelerator speeds up electrons to the superhigh energy needed to study things smaller than an atom. Unlike most high schoolers, Peggy had no problem explaining this complex and powerful technology to visitors. Even if she didn't always know the answers, Peggy never felt nervous about having to talk about such complicated concepts. Most of the time, due to her understanding of physics, she could answer people's questions. Other times, she might ask her father or go right to the *Encyclopedia Britannica* or a real dictionary—which she still loves and uses today. (Take that, internet!) With the knowledge and practice as an explainer, Peggy grew more confident—even if she didn't always realize it.

Atoms, Electrons, and Accelerators

All things are made up of atoms, the basic units of matter. They are broken down into particles: protons, neutrons, and electrons, and even smaller bits called quarks. After the big bang occurred 13.8 billion years ago, the universe cooled, and quarks and electrons formed. Quarks then formed protons and neutrons and combined into nuclei. As the universe cooled and the electrons slowed, it took 380,000 years for them to be trapped around the nuclei, forming atoms.

Now that scientists understand that atoms are the building blocks of matter, they have figured out how to use technology to manipulate them for different purposes. The Stanford two-mile linear accelerator increases the speed of electrons in order for researchers to study the structure of molecules. Other accelerators can create beams that are used to fight cancer, kill bacteria, develop better materials for diapers, and make vehicles more energy efficient. Or . . . bake a potato in about one millisecond!

During the 1960s and '70s, American women fought for equal rights at home and at the workplace. Peggy remembers an inappropriate comment made by a man visiting the Exploratorium. She ignored him. Sexism against women in science exists, yet over the years she's learned to make the best of her situation—no matter what obstacles or barriers may be placed in front of her. To her core, she feels that we all should be treated equally, regardless of race, gender, or intelligence, and that is how she lives her life. In today's world, Peggy notices when women are treated unfairly and will push back and call out sexist comments. We deserve equality, she believes. That's how the world should work.

Three Waves of Feminism

During the twentieth century, three waves of feminism have demonstrated the evolution of women's rights in the United States. Inspired by abolitionists and the Seneca Falls Convention of 1848 (and Frederick Douglass's support), the first wave, which led to the women's suffrage movement, focused on women's rights to own property, defying "ownership" of women in marriage, and the right to vote—which resulted in the passage of the Nineteenth Amendment in 1920, securing them this right.

During Peggy's years in high school and college, the United States was moving through its second wave of feminism (1960s–1980s). This movement addressed the unequal cultural and political opportunities for women. It focused on how opportunities for a woman's personal life might be unfair and force her into a limited identity. In 1963, activist and writer Betty Friedan wrote *The Feminine Mystique*, a book that criticizes the norm that women need to be mothers, wives, and homemakers in order to be happy. These ideas changed social expectations worldwide, accepting women as they find their own identities.

In the early 1990s, the third wave of feminism challenged the definition of femininity and highlighted how race, ethnicity, class, religion, gender, and nationality all play a part in the search for equity in women's lives. This wave celebrated these diverse factors among women. The movement, which continues today, began to break down boundaries that reinforce systemic injustice and discrimination, especially for people of color and people living beyond society's cisgender-hetero norms.

When observing people and the environment in the natural world, Peggy finds all kinds of interesting things to "see, feel, experience, notice." Today, most people spend their time interacting with computer or smartphone screens, but Peggy feels that relishing nature with all the senses, experiencing both the small and big things around us and within us, is the most important way to live. Today, many kids don't have much free time. They're busy with extracurricular activities. She believes kids need time to play on their own or to just think, to be innovative and look at the world with a critical eye.

As a child, Peggy enjoyed discovering things in nature, like rocks and birds. She thought about them and asked questions that sparked curiosity. Peggy believes that grown-ups should allow kids to form their own questions instead of telling them what to think. Throughout her young life, Peggy was not specifically encouraged to go into science, but she was never discouraged. Her parents didn't push her in any one direction. Yet their encouragement and example went a long way.

Science runs in Peggy's blood. Out of the seven kids in her family, five studied math or science, and two of her siblings have incorporated science into their careers as elementary school teachers. Two of her nieces and her own daughter studied in STEM-related fields. Plus, her niece, Marianne Karplus, is an earthquake scientist who is constantly inspired by her Aunt Peggy (and also featured in this book!).

At the University of California San Diego, Peggy majored in physics, which allowed her to study some pretty cool stuff about how the world works. She spent her junior year abroad and completed her bachelor's degree in 1973. Later, she returned to Germany, the place of her childhood memories, for a master's degree in physics at the University of Göttingen.

Afterward, Peggy took her first turn toward earthquake science at the seismological laboratory of Germany's Federal Institute for Geosciences and Natural Resources. By then she'd gotten married and started a family, so she worked part-time writing computer programs and processing data. All the while, though, she began figuring out seismology—diving into how seismometers worked and learning about earthquakes at the same time. With practice and studying, Peggy's knowledge about seismology grew. She learned about earthquake history of the world and California's quake history as well.

Upon returning to the United States in the mid-1980s, Peggy worked on strong motion earthquake projects at the US Geological Survey. Wanting to be able to lead her own research, Peggy decided to get her doctoral degree through the University of Stuttgart in Germany, in 2000. Peggy focused her PhD studies on Lascar, a volcano in Chile that is among the most active in the Central Andes. It spews lava, steam, and volcanic gasses. Inside, the volcano shakes with earthquakes and tremors. Peggy's colleagues in Chile recorded these continuous seismic vibrations and sent her the data to study. Through this analysis, she found some weird signals. In her thesis, she made a hypothesis and proposed several different methods of looking at how gases and magma flow inside the bubbling volcano. Using physics and innovation, Peggy was able to define the different sounds she heard by studying the geometry of the sound waves inside the volcano and what was producing the seismic activity. This innovative approach of listening to a volcano produced unique conclusions and impressed her doctoral professors.

Studying seismic data can be difficult because scientists must listen to sounds. Nobody can travel inside a volcano to see what's happening, and Peggy says it's like being a doctor listening to a gurgling stomach, trying to figure out what the person had for dinner. Seismologists hear everything with their instruments, even leaf blowers, airplanes, or a motorcycle racing down the road. Earthquake scientists must decipher these noises without knowing where they come from. Seismologists, like Peggy, are always thinking. Always listening. Always asking why.

Over the years, Peggy has been around the world and learned lots of things. Mostly, she's figured out how to keep herself happy. Peggy believes you should always do something that you love and not pay attention to what others think. What is important, she says, is "what you think about yourself." Make the best decisions you can and don't second-guess yourself. Stay true and live in the present. Look forward instead of back.

Peggy has had her share of struggles, from questioning which direction to take in her life to moving forward when others thought differently. But her goal has always been to help people understand things. After a recent talk she gave about earthquakes, a woman approached her and said, "I finally feel like I understood something!" That's Peggy's goal. To help people better understand the world they live in.

As a mom, Peggy has supported her kids' quest for knowledge and their desire to follow their own interests. Peggy's daughter, who is younger than her brothers, always felt as if she didn't know as much as the boys. With encouragement, Peggy reminded her daughter that girls and boys are equal and that she, too, would learn more as she grew older. She took her son to Greece when he was a preteen. After visiting ancient ruins like Mycenae and showing him the very spot where the famous King Agamemnon was murdered, her son shrugged and said, "It's just rocks." Peggy laughed and wasn't upset that he didn't find the ancient ruins exciting like she did. She always allows her kids be themselves.

Peggy doesn't shy away from being the interesting and fun grandma who shares her love of the natural world with her grandkids. She recently took a road trip in her camper with her young granddaughters. Spontaneously, they stopped along the roadside near Mount Rushmore to examine a group of sparkly rocks. The girls thought they were fantastic! Like her own father, Peggy asked the girls how they thought these rocks formed. She valued their answers, and without them knowing it, was teaching them to think for themselves.

Peggy is always listening, thinking, and making the world a better place. And she's a pretty cool daughter too. For her mother's 85th birthday, Peggy and other family members got together and raised money to build a library in a small town in Jamaica, the place where her mom had lived during her time in the Peace Corps—complete with computers and over 1,500 books. As their project manager, Peggy guided her family members through the process to honor their mother and give back to a community in need.

She is an everyday hero who works to arm as many people as possible with earthquake warning systems. Her biggest contribution is being an interface between science and the people who need to understand and believe that science is accessible to all. Peggy is hopeful and doesn't dwell on what could happen in the future. She's confident that scientists will continue to learn how to better prepare for each seismic event. Peggy will be there to do what she can, continuing to help us listen to what's happening under the earth, explain our world, and protect lives.

Peggy's Top Three Tips for Earthquake Safety

Make sure you have some cash available as cash machines won't work.

Have an earthquake party every year to use up your supplies, then replenish them. If you don't want to use your supplies for a party, think about reimagining them—you will like them better in case of a quake.

Have a plan and figure out how this plan can be adapted to work for other emergencies you might experience.

Debbie Weiser:
Saving the World Through Science

Throughout her life, Dr. Debbie Weiser's friends have enjoyed her "nerdy love" for geology and earthquakes, even though they might have rolled their eyes once or twice. She learns by interacting with nature—saving her tentmate from a caterpillar or giving friends a lesson on how to "pee in the woods." Debbie is the go-to geologist when someone needs to know about a geological formation and even inspired her parents to take a geology class, since they couldn't always have a "pocket Debbie" with them when they traveled. But mainly, Debbie has always loved earthquakes, and this curiosity led her to creating all sorts of quake-related projects in school. Being hooked on seismology at such a young age only fueled her fire to know more.

At first, as an undergraduate geology student at Occidental College in Los Angeles, and then later as a doctoral student in geology at the University of California, Los Angeles (UCLA), Debbie learned not only to find ways to engage in her passion, but also to seek out opportunities that opened doors. By traveling the globe on research teams, Debbie has gained the wisdom she needs to be good at her job. In graduate school, she visited China to study past earthquakes and learned quickly that young women could be discouraged or devalued in science. Being dropped into a community just a few months after a big quake humbled her, and she learned the value of using science to comfort people and make their lives better.

After 10 years working as a student geologist with the US Geological Survey (USGS), Debbie first became a customer success strategist and then senior manager of customer success with One Concern, a company that uses technology to help people prepare for and lessen the risk of disasters. Continuing to work around the world, she spent time in Mexico City just two weeks after the magnitude 7.1 quake killed 225 people and leveled 44 buildings in 2017. The sorrow she witnessed spurred her to make things safer for people in the future. Through her research in postquake Alaska and in the desert town of Ridgecrest, California, Debbie has come to understand that after devastating trauma, those affected must be allowed to tell their story to start the healing process. Debbie leaves a piece of her heart in every place she visits.

Debbie believes that through education and advanced technology, early warning systems will be in place before the next Big One hits. With more funding, research, and support from governments, and with the enthusiasm of experts like Debbie, early warning technology can be more reliable and accurate. Whether walking her rescue dog Buddy or working to comfort community members in a disaster, Debbie is always looking for ways to make lives better. Her family jokes that she's going to "save the world with science." Debbie is grateful for the opportunity to help others and feels empowered by work that betters society and reduces risks.

As a kid, Debbie was afraid of the usual things, like dark nights or the rumor a giant squid lived in the waters near her home. But after experiencing her first significant earthquake at age 10, instead of feeling afraid, she was curious. Debbie asked her parents if she could feel one again. She wanted to know more about quakes. In middle school, she took a class for kids about earthquake science called "Shake, Rattle, and Roll" at the local university. She then centered all her school projects around quakes, tsunamis, and the Ring of Fire, a path along the Pacific Ocean with high volcanic and earthquake activity.

The Giant Squid of Seattle

Myths about a giant squid, or the Seattle kraken, lurking under the surface of the Pacific Ocean off the state of

Washington, have been repeated through many generations. This mythical sea monster was part of Nordic folk-
lore almost a thousand years ago. The kraken, possibly
the biggest monster of the time, was said to patrol the
seas around Norway, Iceland, and Greenland, where it
pulled ships underwater with its multiple arms or caused
deadly whirlpools.

But fantasy and reality often coincide. The kraken was
first given a scientific name in 1857, classifying it as a
cephalopod in same the family as octopuses, squid, and
cuttlefish. The largest giant squid recorded by scientists
measures about 43 feet long, with half of that length
being its long, agile tentacles. Because kraken have a
deep-sea habitat, scientists are forced to study parts of
the giant squid that are washed up on beaches, found in
the stomach of sperm whales, or dragged up by fishing
gear. Once in a while, though, one of Debbie's nightmares
might be caught on video . . . cruising along in the dark
depths of the sea.

While in ninth grade, after working on a year-long research
project on school earthquake safety, she remembers peeking
outside her classroom door. Debbie thought she was hearing
construction noise, but it turned out to be the sounds of an
earthquake's first arriving waves, or P waves. She hopped under

her desk as the shaking began, her mind racing with thoughts of her research come to life. Afterward, she realized that she had *heard* the sound generated by P waves *before* feeling the earth shake.

Years later, during her first year of grad school, she was hanging out with a small group of friends when a small earthquake hit. All her friends looked at her like she'd actually made it happen. Many people close to her have become more prepared and earthquake-ready. And that makes Debbie happy.

In her undergraduate and graduate work, Debbie experienced much of what life might be like as a scientist in the field—the good and bad. She learned a lot about ethics of research, like the time she worked with a professor who had questionable techniques. He brought his family along on research outings and expected her, and other female scientists, to watch his children instead of conducting studies. In grad school, on another field research project in China, the team used paleoseismological methods to describe earthquake history there. The lead scientist was sure he'd found the earthquake fault they'd been searching for, but Debbie disagreed and voiced her opinion. Nobody listened. Eventually, an 80-year-old male scientist came to the same conclusion as Debbie, and they believed him. Being devalued was painful, yet it gave her strength and helped ground her argument. She knew then that as a young woman, she'd have to be confident and put the weight of her belief behind her thinking.

Paleoseismology: Looking Back in Earthquake Time

Who needs a time machine when you have a paleoseismologist around? By gathering data along sections of a fault, scientists can determine the history of an earthquake. Using this data, researchers make predictions to keep structures and people safe during the next shaking. Earthquake detectives look for fault scarps, small steps on the ground where one side of the fault has moved vertically. They also search for folded layers of soil or places in the land that have been lifted, titled, dropped, or torn apart. To find these clues, experts must first locate faults and then find evidence that has been preserved or covered by soil for hundreds or thousands of years. Paleoseismologists mainly uncover indications of larger earthquakes since smaller ones don't leave as much proof.

In her current position, Debbie has not experienced overt gender bias, but she has witnessed others' experiences and still notices mostly male voices on panels and as moderators at conferences. Yet, throughout her studies, Debbie has been surrounded by incredible women and men and feels extremely lucky for the current shift in gender dynamics. In plate tectonics class, she was swept up in the enthusiasm of her engaging professor, Scott Bogue. He made the topic relatable and fostered his students' natural curiosity. This fueled her hunger to know more.

As a sophomore, Debbie attended a talk given by the famous earthquake expert Dr. Lucy Jones. That talk connected all the elements Debbie had been so curious about, helping her realize that she could study earthquakes for a living *and* their impacts on people. She mustered up the confidence to ask Lucy if the USGS was hiring interns, and then the two visited in a coffee shop after. Not only did Lucy hire Debbie as an intern, but afterward, she also took Debbie on at the USGS as a student geologist for 10 years!

At UCLA, Debbie had an incredible graduate advisor, David Jackson, who always encouraged her to figure things out on her own. She learned how to investigate and solve problems using life and coping skills.

Working in the field is full of challenges. Debbie has experienced extremely hot weather, strong winds, changing temperatures, and dust devils. She's had to face many of her fears, like tarantula wasps, which sound like a humming refrigerator, landing on her. Debbie says that the hours are super demanding, but you get to use cool technology and form a close comradery with team members.

In Chile, four to five months after the magnitude 8.8 earthquake killed more than 500 people in 2010, Debbie's team hoped to learn as much as they could about the country's building codes, which were similar to California's. But the disaster was fresh. The 8-to-10-foot tsunami traveled across the Pacific at 450 miles per hour and destroyed entire villages. She spoke to first responders and witnessed coastal communities where hospitals, schools, and homes had been washed away, leaving only the tile flooring and scattered debris. Debbie had a hard time reconciling that many lost their lives because they were in buildings that couldn't withstand the force of the quake and tsunami.

In the middle of the chaos, Debbie's team received seismic information from recovery and governmental organizations doing the challenging work of recording data and assessing the damage and impact on the local people. Many more lives could have been lost in this quake, but people had not forgotten the deadly 1960 magnitude 9.5 earthquake. Lives were saved in 2010 because people remembered the devastation of the 1960 event, the largest ever recorded. It triggered a massive tsunami, killed more than 1,600 people, and left 2 million homeless. People remembered that if the shaking was strong enough to knock you down, a tsunami was coming. This gave them the warning they needed to evacuate.

In the 2010 event, more than 500 displaced families had been housed in temporary shelters. Debbie remembers a mother taking her hands, describing the squalid living conditions (100 people per restroom) and how her young daughters were constantly sick. She said, "Please, I don't want the world to forget us." This raw, powerful experience of someone who had lost so much made Debbie realize the huge responsibility that scientists have to not only record data but also improve safety and help people. Debbie hugged the woman and told her that she would never forget. And Debbie hasn't. In Chile, she has witnessed the efficiency and resilience of community organizations and first responders, the true strength of people, and the love and care of strangers. That's how communities recover.

After graduating with her PhD in geology, Debbie's job search proved difficult. She found a cool company called One Concern, and even though they weren't hiring for her position, she spent hours constructing the perfect three-paragraph e-mail that would show them what she had to offer. They responded quickly and hired her after an interview, although she found out later that she had the job after that one e-mail! Debbie's advice is don't be afraid to ask. If you don't ask, she says, you are rejecting yourself.

With One Concern, Debbie has been all over the world in hopes of helping others see potential hazards. Part of her job is writing reports, but one of her most important duties is to improve and better humanity. And that happens by witnessing postdisaster recovery. Traveling to Mexico City in 2017, just two weeks after a magnitude 7.1 earthquake struck, Debbie recalls walking the streets, talking to people, and seeing a collapsed building where 40 people had died. Lace curtains still blew in the breeze from a blasted window frame, and an unbroken broom stuck out of the rubble. A kid-sized red car was sandwiched between the layers, perfectly preserved. Debbie couldn't help but think that on a normal day, being in the wrong place at the wrong time had caused so many deaths. For her, these experiences drove home the vital need for good building codes and government support. More lives could have been saved.

By documenting what she sees and listening to people's suffering, she can honor both those who perished and those who survived by collecting experiences and capturing data. But Debbie must somehow find peace in these challenging moments. She admits how difficult it is to be standing where somcone has died and remain composed as a scientist doing her job. She must record their stories so others are less likely to go through the same thing. Debbie takes solace in seeing how disasters can bring out the best in many people, how people try to help in ways they are best suited for, like engineers willing to go out and inspect houses for free. Kindness and love can go a long way.

Dr. Hiroo Kanamori: Seismological Groundbreaker

California Institute of Technology's Smits Professor of Geology and winner of the 2007 Kyoto Prize in Basic Sciences, Dr. Hiroo Kanamori has been studying how the earth moves over his lifelong career. In the 1960s, Hiroo made a great discovery noting how all major earthquakes ruptured along the Pacific Rim. Continuing with big contributions in his field, he introduced moment magnitude, which helped measure earthquake strength and further developed the theory of plate tectonics. He also applied his research on the rupture process, decreasing seismic hazards and using advanced technology in the development of real-time tsunami warning systems. He believes that both advancements in data collection and analysis and preparation are the keys to saving lives. This research makes life worth living, he says, "even saving just one life."

North America continues to have its share of quakes. In 2018, Debbie led a team from the University of Alaska Anchorage, after a magnitude 7.0 quake hit Alaska and caused $76 million in damage. Debbie's teams examined building damage inside and outside of Anchorage. Outside the city, they witnessed how building codes were not enforced, and she observed inadequate building practices that left homes literally cracked apart. They also saw the tenacity of the Alaska Department of Transportation employees, who rapidly repaired major damage around the airport. With incessant aftershocks, Debbie noted firsthand the collective strain and posttraumatic stress symptoms in the local people. They were unsure of when the ground would stop shaking, waking them up at night, or whether the next aftershock was really the Big One coming.

Closer to home, on July 4, 2019, Ridgecrest, a small desert town in Southern California, began to shake. From Los Angeles, California, Debbie received the USGS early warning for the magnitude 6.4 earthquake. She felt 20–30 seconds of low-intensity, or low-frequency, ground motion. The shaking was long, but no real damage occurred in L.A. After sheltering in place during the trembling, duty called, and she toted her laptop to three holiday barbecues, working virtually for a total of 17 hours that day. The next morning, she picked up her colleague, a cayenne pepper coffee, and a big breakfast burrito and drove approximately three hours around Ridgecrest doing reconnaissance.

When she got home that night, another magnitude 7.1 quake struck, and Debbie knew she had her work cut out for her. With a team of eight, she returned to Ridgecrest in the 108 degree weather and collected data for two days, walking around neighborhoods to see how buildings had held up. She talked to people, once again witnessing the trauma of the aftershocks. In real time, she got to see a surface rupture, a place where the fault extends up to the surface of the earth, something she'd only seen in photos. Debbie stood there, right off the road, staring at the big crack in the ground, fascinated, but reminded again of the power that nature had over mankind.

Economics plays a huge role in the impact and recovery of a community after a natural disaster. Ridgecrest, a fairly new town, had more updated structures that were built with lower stories as well as more modern homes. The neighboring town of Trona suffered far worse. The main water pipe broke and people had no running water. FEMA (the Federal Emergency Management Agency) sent semitrucks full of bottled water, and the National Guard set up resources at the local high school. With severe damage to the mineral mining plant, the main source of income, this community saw many hard times ahead.

With a huge weight on her shoulders, it's hard for Debbie to balance gathering information and giving back to the people. She acknowledges how important it is that this data gets published and analyzed so that governments and other organizations can plan, minimizing damage during quakes. Experts must get out of their scientist space and engage with politicians to inform them of these changes, make people hear what needs to be done, and help enable decision-making.

Communicating the science from these heart-wrenching experiences will make us all safer, reduce risk, and minimize the number of lives lost. So much needs to be done in risk management, she says, and we are just hitting the tip of the iceberg. Public education is vital, and people must be taught how to use the early warning systems and about building codes and safety.

And people like Debbie can do just that. Through empathy, expertise, and a passion for earthquakes, she helps break down barriers that prevent people from understanding the science. Debbie can assess the damage and help others digest what they need to know in order to keep their family, community, state, and country safer from the inevitable shaking under our feet. There she goes again, saving the world through science.

Debbie's Top Three Tips for Earthquake Safety

Water. First and foremost. Can't survive without it!

Always have a can opener in your emergency kit.

Use your camping supplies after a natural disaster.

Clara Yoon:
An Algorithm of Success

You might find this geophysicist exploring a remote ghost town in the desert, visiting an art museum in Paris, or at home collecting stuffed animals like Hello Kitty. As a lifelong Californian, Dr. Clara Yoon has lived through many earthquakes that were "equally scary and fascinating," which became a big part of her inspiration to study earth sciences. With many fields of expertise, Clara is a mathematician and worked for years in the defense industry as a computer programmer where she did "secret work that you can't talk about in the outside world."

Switching careers midway in life, Clara earned her PhD in geophysics and took a job at the US Geological Survey (USGS) where she could help reduce the risk of earthquakes to society. She developed software and computer operations that monitored seismic activity in Southern California, and recently moved into research to find solutions to questions about how quakes start, stop, and interact with each other. In her career, she must communicate, collaborate, and innovate, and Clara has inspired other scientists to look outside the traditional methods in geophysics; she was part of a team that created a special algorithm to detect small earthquakes based on other popular apps.

Performing her magic behind a computer screen, Clara worked extensively on the response to the magnitude 6.4 and 7.1 2019 Ridgecrest earthquake sequence on July 4 in Southern California, which was felt by almost 50,000 people as far away as Northern California and Arizona. Studying quakes in the Midwest, a region not normally associated with seismic activity until a decade ago, Clara looked at data that led to unexpected results. Human activity from the oil and gas industry is thought to be causing these earthquakes. Clara identified small earthquakes in Arkansas that had been induced by hydraulic fracturing, or "fracking," the practice of injecting high-pressure fluid into rock layers to extract more oil. Clara says that although modern society relies on oil and gas for energy, ways to cheaply produce these resources must be weighed against the potential risk of earthquakes. Clara's job at the USGS is to communicate this vital information honestly and accurately to the public in order to keep people safe. With her knowledge and drive, Clara's hope is to become an expert resource on earthquakes using cutting-edge technology.

But dreams like this don't come without a struggle. As the child of immigrants from South Korea, Clara said she fit that "uncool nerdy Asian stereotype" and struggled to overcome social isolation. Life got better, Clara says, when she began to take risks, dive into her passions, and find close connections to others. She believes more diversity is needed in STEM fields, and advises girls to learn the ropes early, find your support network, and become an advocate for yourself. Clara thinks outside the box and works more than she needs to. Why? Because she wants to save lives, and by doing something she loves, she can do just that.

Clara grew up with parents who valued education and encouraged her to pursue a career in STEM. With unusual interests as a young girl, her imagination ran wild with thoughts of irrational numbers and the periodic table of elements. She collected rocks and minerals and was fascinated by the vastness of the universe and elementary particles such as quarks. Math and science came easy, and her parents were unfamiliar with "traditional" girl activities like sleepovers, Girl Scouts, or sports. Clara felt lonely until she started to find activities that challenged her. She joined the Academic Decathlon and Science Olympiad, and at age 12 got to fly on a plane for the first time to travel to a competition.

She remembers earthquakes during her childhood all too well, especially the magnitude 6.7 in Northridge, California—10–12 seconds of the strongest shaking she's ever felt. This quake destroyed thousands of buildings and cost more than $20 billion in damage. It killed 57 people, injured 9,000, and displaced more than 20,000. Clara lived safely 60 miles away from the epicenter but will never forget pictures of the twisted metal and smashed concrete where entire floors of buildings disappeared, and many people died. She remembers seeing the collapsed freeway footage on TV, which still haunts her when she drives by that area. Little did she know that while these disasters were taking place, she was inspired to become someone who would answer unsolved questions and help prevent destruction and loss of life.

As a quiet and shy kid, she didn't fit in with mainstream American norms. Eventually, she learned to accept and appreciate her understanding of how it felt to come from an immigrant family plus be the odd person out, the girl who loved math and science but couldn't find anyone else to relate to. This outsider perspective, Clara believes, helped propel her into science and embrace questioning widely accepted assumptions about science and society in general.

After graduating with a degree in physics and a minor in math from the University of California, Los Angeles, Clara took the first job offered to her, in the defense industry, where she used radar science and remote sensing to map the earth's surface. This technology emits radio waves from an antenna on a plane or satellite, which then bounce off different structures on the earth's surface and return to their source. The length and strength of their return, analyzed with computer software, help scientists figure out what's on the ground.

Clara liked computer programming and writing software, but her boyfriend (now husband) was a geology major and met with other geologists and earth scientists on field trips. To Clara, it seemed they were having way more fun than computer programmers, which inspired her to go back to school to get a graduate degree in geophysics. Two more quakes also reinforced her passion to learn more: the 2010 magnitude 7.2 El Mayor-Cucapah quake in Baja California, Mexico, which left 35,000 people without homes and destroyed massive agricultural areas, plus the deadly 2011 magnitude 9.0 Tohoku, Japan, quake, which led to 20,000 deaths and 500,000 displaced people. Once again, tragedy motivated Clara to want to know more.

Earning her master's degree and her PhD in geophysics at Stanford University allowed Clara to combine physics, math, earth science, and computer programming, in which she learned a new computer language called Python. She took earth science and seismology classes, conducted original research, and wrote a 200-page thesis. Wow!

By recognizing tiny earthquake patterns, scientists can identify previously unknown earthquakes, figure out where they are located underground, and better understand how to find faults deep within the earth. To compare "wiggle patterns" of tiny earthquakes to a larger set of samples, Clara's team developed the Fingerprint and Similarity Thresholding (FAST) algorithm, which is similar to methods used to create the music recognition app, Shazam. It worked and inspired other scientists to use innovation to make new discoveries.

Speak Like a Computer

In order to speak or give instructions to a computer, a programmer can use a variety of different programming languages to communicate efficiently. Each type of computer programming language, like Python that Clara mentioned, may have common or varying features, just like human languages. Programming languages serve a variety of purposes, whether to engineer computer software more easily or to create apps for smartphones. Programming languages allow us to direct processing power to our needs. With the aid and guidance of these languages, computers can efficiently process massive amounts of information, much faster than any human.

Clara was in the right place at the right time when a research scientist job became available at the USGS. In this position, she continues to explore the unknown and believes that every earthquake is an opportunity to learn something new. In Southern California, Clara's lucky to work in an air-conditioned office where she has the freedom to dive into important research topics on her own schedule. Working as a geophysicist, she analyzes recordings of ground motion from different earthquakes using sensitive instruments, and she writes software that helps find tiny faults deep underground. As she writes an application program, she must include math instructions that allow the computer to determine where the quake started, the characteristics of the rocks underground, and how they moved on either side of the fault. She tells the computer to draw pictures of earthquake information, which may look like a pattern of wiggles showing how violently the quake shook the ground, or a map of the location of the faults. Instead of roughing it in the field in 100-degree heat, Clara can use technology to uncover patterns and information that reveal these seismic mysteries.

The Superstar San Andreas Fault Zone

Experts believe that the infamous San Andreas fault zone in California started moving around 30 million years ago and has "slipped," meaning one side of the fault has moved passed the other side, more than 200 miles. Displacement along the fault in 1906 produced the great San Francisco earthquake, originally reported to have killed 700 people, but that number is now thought to be three to four times worse. As the boundary between the Pacific and North American tectonic plates, the main San Andreas fault (and some parallel faults) run 800 miles from Southern to Northern California. Scientists gather data along sections of the fault to figure out the details of past earthquakes, and this information reveals that in some spots, the state is overdue for the Big One.

On her first weeklong shift as a seismologist, Clara felt slight shaking while at home on the Fourth of July holiday. She was on 24-hour call for the Southern California Seismic Network. At first, she thought it was a truck passing by, but then her pager blared, showing a magnitude 6.4 in Ridgecrest, a small city in the desert. Clara made phone calls to other experts in federal and state government and dealt with the news media outside her office. But the activity wasn't over. The next day, the earth shook again—this time for 10 seconds. Her pager beeped again, displaying a magnitude 7.1 quake, even bigger than the day before. Via phone, she again answered questions from reporters about the possibility of the Big One that could happen next along the San Andreas. Her pager continued to blare as aftershock after aftershock shook the earth, and when the earth finally settled, Clara's work didn't stop. The 2019 magnitude 6.4 and 7.1 Ridgecrest quakes were the largest to be felt in the Southern California area in the last 10 years.

She attended meetings, was interviewed by more reporters, gave aftershock updates, and wrote reports about the automatic ShakeMap, or real-time ground shaking intensity map. But mostly, she learned that as a seismologist, her most important duty was to communicate reliable, accurate information about the quake to the public. This "new sense of purpose" inspired her to work even harder to determine the cause of the Ridgecrest quakes and what it means for seismic hazards in other communities. Clara has never looked back about her decision to change careers at a later stage in her life. If she hadn't taken time to pursue her passion, she would have had regrets. And so far, it's been totally worth it.

Clara would never describe her path into seismology as smooth or easy, yet she has gained much wisdom. Growing up, she didn't really know the steps to take in order to become a scientist, and she felt "not knowing what you don't know" held her back. This path can be hidden to people who don't personally know scientists, and today, Clara wants to be a guide for kids (and adults). It's possible to learn this scientific culture—how to talk to famous professors, behave at conferences, get the education and knowledge you need, and present your research—you just have to work at it. She advises girls and young people to start early and take advanced math and science in middle and high school. And remember that when you are learning something new, it's OK not to understand it the first time. Science can be challenging, Clara says, "but there are no stupid questions." Eventually, she believes, you will get it. Ask for help, and don't give up!

Wastewater Injection and Fracking

Fracking, or hydraulic fracturing, is a technique used by companies to extract natural gas or oil from rock more easily. To crack the rock, they blast water, chemicals, and sand into it, allowing gas or oil to flow to the surface.

Wastewater injection is a process used for disposing of these waste fluids. Although reports of fracking-caused earthquakes are rare, wastewater injections can induce earthquakes. Most wastewater injection wells are not the cause of earthquakes that are felt by people, but scientists are still studying how this human-made action below the earth may affect earthquake events and people on the surface.

Clara says young women must learn how to negotiate and advocate for themselves because "working hard, pleasing others, not causing a fuss, and hoping to get noticed by your boss" won't help them advance in their career. All the raises and promotions Clara has received were a result of her asking for them. Keep a list of your accomplishments, she advises, and know how to communicate your value. Don't be afraid to ask for help, because it is a sign of strength.

"Earthquakes don't give up their secrets easily," Clara says, and she still deals with doubt. As a researcher, sometimes Clara conducts experiments that don't work or writes computer programs that don't produce the right answer. Yet she enjoys this unknown journey that hopefully leads her to a new discovery or way of thinking. She's much more comfortable in the STEM world than when she was a young girl. In college, she studied with both girls and guys who were in it "for the love of physics" and who helped each other out. "I felt like I belonged," she recalls, as many of her peers came from immigrant families or backgrounds where they were the first in their families to pursue scientific or professional careers. She's been fortunate to have worked with so many positive and supportive people in earthquake science—even amazing professors that measured their own success by the success of their students.

Sadly, she also acknowledges the other side of the coin where women have been discouraged or pushed out of science due to harassment, bullying, isolation, or lack of mentoring. This is not acceptable to Clara. Throughout her experience, she's witnessed many women help each other out but hasn't seen as many people of color or those with diverse economic backgrounds in earthquake science, even in California, an extremely diverse state. She wants the future to mark these changes. Clara hopes to help others succeed in their scientific careers like her mentors helped her, especially younger and newer scientists.

To stay healthy, Clara takes good care of herself first before she can care for others, and is extremely grateful for her husband, a former geologist, who inspires her as well. As an immigrant from Mexico, he grew up in a low-income family in Los Angeles and was the first person in his family to finish high school and go to college. Clara admires how he overcame so many obstacles. She loves living in Southern California with her husband and young son and is fascinated with the geological features in the area. Culturally, Clara loves the richness in Los Angeles, a city with many immigrants, in addition to its art, entertainment, restaurants, and great weather. She's especially drawn to places like the Sierra Nevada mountains and Mojave Desert, where she loves to explore remote dirt roads, sand dunes, and old ruins—and marvel at the granite mountains and deep blue lakes.

Clara loves to travel and meet interesting people from around the globe, and she's learned that science as a lifestyle is better than she ever imagined. Through exploration and collaboration, she's realized how important it is to seek the truth and come up with stories to explain these observations. Clara hopes that more people get the opportunity to study science . . . or whatever their calling may be. Clara lives and breathes earthquakes. And she wouldn't have it any other way.

Clara's Top Three Tips for Earthquake Safety

When you feel shaking drop, cover, hold on. Try to get under a table and protect your head and neck. Wait for the shaking to stop. Don't run outside. Expect aftershocks.

Before the earthquake happens: Prepare emergency supplies for you and your family. Go to www.earthquakecountry.org for the full list of supplies you need.

If a quake happens during the day, make a plan for a meeting location.

Follow Clara Yoon Online:

Website: http://www.usgs.gov/staff-profiles/clara-yoon and
https://www.its.caltech.edu/~cyoon/

Twitter: @Qlara999

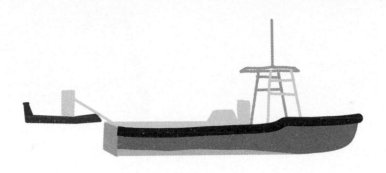

Part II

In the Field:
On Land, at Sea, and in Volcanoes

Lori Dengler: Waves of Information

In 2011, a small fishing boat drifted across the Pacific Ocean and became beached in Crescent City, California, after the magnitude 9.0 Tohoku earthquake and tsunami hit Japan. For geologist Dr. Lori Dengler, the boat became an opportunity to connect people on both sides of the Pacific, as well as a tool to build people's tsunami resilience.

For nearly 40 years, this emeritus professor of geology and Scholar of the Year at Humboldt State University in California has used her global expertise in tsunami and earthquake hazards to build preparedness programs in California. In places like Papua New Guinea, Indonesia, Chile, and Japan, she has studied in posttsunami research teams and witnessed firsthand the impact, trauma, and recovery of communities in these regions. With this data and eyewitness survival stories, she works to help coastal Californians prepare and stay safe during future seismic events. Lori's approach is to build grassroots networks of government agencies, preparedness organizations, and businesses to educate communities about the seismic risks along California's northern coast, the most seismically active region of the state, which has suffered more frequent tsunami damage than any other area of the West Coast.

Six weeks after the Japanese tsunami of 2011, Lori was part of a field team that visited the hardest hit areas. Two years later, her connections from that experience helped to link Crescent City in California's northernmost county to Rikuzentakata, Japan, after a small tsunami debris boat named *Kamome* (seagull) was found in Del Norte County. In 2018, Rikuzentakata and Crescent City became sister cities.

Lori was part of the group that developed the US National Tsunami Hazard Mitigation Program in 1996, and she wrote the original plan for this program. In 2004, she codirected the effort to revise UNESCO's Intergovernmental Oceanographic Commission's posttsunami field survey guide. Her passion is research, collaboration, and projects that more effectively communicate earthquake and tsunami safety. Her projects not only connect people worldwide through struggle, but they also prevent tragedy and loss of life from the mysterious shaking under the earth.

Coming from an academic family, education was always a part of Lori's life. Both her parents played musical instruments, and her grandfather was a university professor. She says that it was expected that all the kids in her family would go to college. Her parents encouraged Lori to find her own path. They ran a travel company and guest ranch in Rancho Mirage, California, where Lori grew a lifelong interest in travel and a fascination with people of all ages. There, she learned that if you want to find something out, find the oldest woman in the room, "ask questions and listen." Her parents never pushed her in one direction, but she was a good student—especially at math. However, Lori felt embarrassed about it because during the 1960s, math was a boy thing and girls who were good at it were definitely uncool.

She arrived at the University of California, Berkley, in 1964, just in time for the free speech movement, in which college students challenged Berkeley's regulations on their political activity and organization. Lori says she discovered geophysics by accident or serendipity. Never being encouraged to go into science, she stayed as far away from those classes in high school as possible and began college as a humanities field major, a mixture of history and art. During her sophomore year, she took a geology class to fulfill the general education science requirement. There were more than 300 students in the class, which was taught by Professor Howell Williams, a volcanologist. He was the first to explain how volcanoes worked in the Cascade Range, which stretched from Canada to Northern California. He taught his students to look at science as an art and that appreciating the aesthetics of the earth was just as important as knowing chemistry or calculus. That blew Lori away.

This was the dawn of the plate tectonics era. A variety of data was coming together that confirmed our planet's surface was not static but had been reshaping itself over most of its history. More precise models of the earth's structure, which came partly from underground nuclear testing, gave a new form to the theory of how continents shift position. This was an exciting time to study the earth, and Lori wanted in.

Geology was fun! The field trips were great, plus she "developed a crush" on the teacher's assistant in her lab class and worked hard to have plenty of intelligent questions to pester him with. The more effort she put into geology, the more interesting it became. Lori had never planned to switch majors, but luckily, she had enough math in high school to jump right into calculus. Even though math was never her favorite class, Lori took it one step at a time and found success through her hard work. In a graduate math class several years later, she even received one of the few As in the course.

As a woman in the sciences, Lori experienced limitations. At this time, the UC Berkeley earth science program discouraged women from majoring in geology and didn't allow them to attend field camp, so she decided on geophysics.

Opportunities like this have changed for women in geology, yet Lori acknowledges that everyone experiences subtle and not-so-subtle discouragement, regardless of their background. She had several professors who treated female students differently and were either blatantly sexist or "closet sexists." In her first quarter of graduate school at a different university, Lori had an advisor who did not like working with women and discouraged her from asking him for help. By being shunned this way, she felt disconnected and discouraged, so much so that she left the school and returned to UC Berkeley to complete her PhD program in geophysics, where she felt much more supported. Lori never forgot the encouragement of her favorite geology professor, John Verhoeven, who taught her to ask questions and develop the logical steps to answer them, a skill she grew throughout her lifetime.

In her career, she has found travel to be one of the best ways to make connections and view the natural world through new lenses. In each new place she visits, Lori jumps into the regional geology and asks questions with a keen scientific eye that allows her to marvel at the world and learn how the earth works. Lori believes that traveling, one of her passions, is the best way to challenge assumptions and think differently. She is forever grateful to have been able to visit extraordinary places for posttsunami field surveys—places she had barely heard of, where she witnessed the impact of a disaster in real time and experienced the resilience of people as they recover. She's gone full circle with her early interest in human culture as an undergrad to now studying postdisaster recovery. Through her fieldwork, Lori has learned that understanding human cultures and behavior is as essential as the physics of processes in reducing the impacts of a natural disaster. You cannot learn that from equations or models. Increasingly, Lori has collaborated with social scientists in much of her work.

Women have nearly achieved parity, the state of being equal, with men in many areas of the earth sciences, but racial balance has lagged. A National Center for Science and Engineering Statistics study in 2015 called the geosciences the *least* diverse of all the science, technology, engineering, and math (STEM) fields. During her 55-year career, she has never considered herself a racist, but Lori says she needs to "fess up—I was part of the problem and like almost all of my geoscience colleagues, the state of our discipline is our fault." Lori believes complacency is the enemy of science and what is needed is "out-of-the-box thinkers." Different backgrounds lead to new perspectives and ways of thinking. Lori says that within every STEM field, we need the entire bandwidth of human abilities to make change in this world. To work toward equity, every community must feel they have a stake in science and how it contributes to their lives. (Lori recommends *How to Be an Antiracist* by Ibram X. Kendi.)

Preparing for earthquakes and tsunamis is at the core of Lori's work. Knowledge is power, and the more we understand these events and how they affect human societies, the better we can inform the emergency response community and grow connections between businesses, government agencies, tribes, etc. With technological advancements in detection, analysis, and communication, Lori believes that earthquake early warning systems, like the US Geological Survey's ShakeAlert in California, Oregon, and Washington, and deep ocean detection of tsunamis are game changers; there will be a time when people routinely get notifications ahead of time. The challenge, however, will be to help them understand and respond.

Over the course of Lori's career, advancements in tsunami warning systems have given scientists a much better understanding of how they work. Deep ocean sensors that sit on the seafloor can now collect much clearer data about a tsunami's source. Warning centers have created grid systems that map likely source areas of big earthquakes. When a big quake hits, scientists can run tsunami models that forecast what water heights at coastal areas will be within 20 minutes of the event.

However, prioritizing earthquake and tsunami warnings does worry Lori, as people tend to forget the threat as time passes, reducing the funding and education needed to keep safe. One of her missions in Northern California is to get people to care about a potential devastating tsunami.

Tsunami Science

Eighty percent of tsunamis are a result of an earthquake beneath the seafloor. Faults deform the seafloor, causing the entire water column above it to raise or lower. This produces water surges that travel outward in every direction. Tsunamis can also be caused by landslides, volcanoes, or certain types of extreme weather.

A tsunami's speed depends on the depth of the ocean. In a very deep ocean, the waves can travel 500 miles per hour or more. Tsunami surges can continue for hours or days, and the largest waves are usually tens of minutes to hours after the first one hits. Tsunamis can affect people close to the source or thousands of miles away.

If you are close to the source, you will feel an earthquake. Large magnitude earthquakes—magnitude 7 and larger—cause tsunamis. The shaking will last a long time, in some cases more than a minute. Even if the shaking isn't strong, its duration is the key that a tsunami could be on its way. Today, much of the West Coast of the United States features tsunami hazard zone road signs. If you are in one of the zones during an earthquake, move inland or to higher ground as soon as you can. Don't wait for official warnings, as earthquake damage may disrupt communications systems.

As a geophysicist, Lori has been a part of eight post-earthquake and tsunami survey teams in both Northern California and abroad—places like Papua New Guinea, Peru, Indonesia, Samoa, Chile, and Japan. Her most difficult field experience was her first. It took her to Papua New Guinea after the magnitude 7.1 quake in 1998. The country was in disarray, plus the scale of the damage and the newness of this raw experience of disaster made it extremely tough on her. Three deadly tsunamis followed the shaking, destroying three of the four villages, killing at least 1,600 people, injuring 1,000, and displacing 10,000 more. Lori says it was gut-wrenching witnessing survivors digging graves and placing simple crucifixes and piles of the victims' belongings, such as soccer balls, children's clothes, and cooking utensils, at their resting place. Earthquakes strong enough to be felt were common in the area, but tsunamis were rare, and few people associated the shaking with a warning sign. Lori believes that almost everyone could have been saved if they had known to move inland.

Earthquakes and tsunamis don't take vacations, and disaster may strike at any time or any place. Lori learned that residents of places where past tsunamis struck are better able to survive them. After the December 27, 2004, magnitude 9.1 earthquake in Indonesia, the deadliest tsunami in recorded history claimed 230,000 lives worldwide. As part of her Indonesian posttsunami field survey in March 2005, Lori visited the hardest hit coastal areas of Northern Sumatra and nearby offshore islands. In most of the area, the loss of life was horrific, with fewer than 10 percent of coastal residents surviving. An exception was Simeulue, an island off the coast of the Indonesian province of Aceh. Langi Village on the northern tip of the island was the closest community to the earthquake's epicenter. The tsunami surges arrived just eight minutes after the quake. Lori expected the losses to be even worse than at the Aceh coast. The tsunami measured 30 to 45 feet high, and Langi was destroyed, but Lori recalls how nobody died because they had kept alive the memories of the last big tsunami a century before. The off-the-grid villagers recognized that the shaking was a warning, so they grabbed children, put their elderly and sick in garden carts, and headed to high ground, where they remained for over a week. The village hadn't experienced a deadly tsunami in five generations, yet the oral traditions kept awareness high.

But often, economic disparities can leave people more vulnerable in disasters. In many developing countries, rural people move to urban areas yet are forced to live in unstable places, like weak hillsides or crowded slums with little access to higher ground. Earthquakes and tsunamis have not increased, Lori says, but what has changed is the population density. With more people living in vulnerable areas, Lori says that the risk is increasing.

People and Disaster Recovery

Economics and resources often determine how a society bounces back from disaster. One study from the University of Oklahoma looked at the recovery of two communities after the 1992 Cape Mendocino earthquake in California that caused 98 injuries, landslides, and damage to infrastructure costing approximately $66 million. Two communities, similar in size and distance from the epicenter, fared differently. Ferndale resident's had higher incomes, more college degrees, and community organizations, while Rio Dell had more low-income residents on welfare and fewer social groups.

A year after the quake, Ferndale nearly recovered and had suffered no significant changes, while Rio Dell was still struggling and in worse shape than before the quake. Economic disparities in postdisaster recovery can only be changed through education, funding, and community efforts. That's why Lori works so hard. That's why she does what she does.

Sometimes, however, disasters bring people together. The small Japanese boat that beached itself at Crescent City had made its way across the Pacific after the 2011 tsunami, which sent ocean waters racing across land, flooding 200 square miles of coastal land with waves almost 125 feet tall. The boat, covered with Japanese writing, barnacles, and mussels, had Japanese characters that read TAKATA HIGH SCHOOL, and a colleague of Lori's who spoke Japanese determined the boat was from a high school in Rikuzentakata. Lori had visited the city during her 2011 posttsunami field survey and followed the city's Facebook page to document recovery efforts. After the *Kamome* was found, she posted photos of the boat on Rikuzentakata's Facebook page, which began a sequence of events that connected high school students an ocean apart, led to student exchanges, and finally a sister city relationship between Crescent City and Rikuzentakata.

Residents discovered that both towns—thousands of miles apart—had a lot in common: both were located along the Pacific coast with fishing industries and towering trees. Students at Del Norte County High School began restoring *Kamome*. Del Norte County students, staff, and city officials collaborated with Rikuzentakata, along with the US and Japanese embassies, to return it to its home.

Lori says that it took many people, from different organizations, to make it all happen, which boggles her mind. Today, the sister relationship is thriving. It took a village, with a little bit of coincidence and miracle thrown in, to reach out and create beauty out of the sadness. Lori says the *Kamome* story is so much better than fiction and is now a documentary titled simply *Kamome*.

By weaving global survival stories into her earthquake and tsunami outreach, Lori can share her message with the public. As a writer, Lori feels that stories are what get people's attention and she believes what works best for her is a personal connection to what she writes. Besides Lori's picture book *The Extraordinary Voyage of Kamome*, she has written a preparedness guidebook called *Living on Shaky Ground*. She also pens a weekly column called "Not My Fault" for Times-Standard.com, mostly about everything earthquakes and tsunamis, but also on a range of topics from climate change to volcanoes, racism in STEM to living during COVID-19.

Lori thinks outside the box. Her passion for spreading disaster education through storytelling has many faces. She's worked with theater companies that reenacted disaster scenarios and inspired an undergraduate student to write a symphony capturing the power of wave inundation after the 2004 Indian Ocean event.

Through her outreach, Lori says that communities have opened their ears and more residents are preparing for future disasters. And after the 2011 Tohoku tsunami, which destroyed boats and Crescent City's harbor (5,000 miles across the Pacific), and produced one of only two deaths outside of Japan, people are paying attention. Through school visits, field trips, or even displays and presentations at county fairs, Lori is convinced that she can reach people and teach them how to prepare for an earthquake or tsunami. Sometimes, Lori admits she doesn't feel like she's making enough progress, but in the end, she gets people talking. And as the late Professor Dennis Mileti said, talking is the first step in getting people to take preparedness actions.

To girls, Lori tries to convey that science is fun and a way to be like Hermione from the Harry Potter books in the real world.

She's been married for more than 40 years and has three amazing children. Lori feels very lucky to have had a life partner for so long who has supported her and never questioned her academic career. It is possible to follow your dreams and have a family. Sometimes, life can get messy. But, if you are like Lori, you will find a way through it, never give up, and make a difference at home—and around the world.

Lori's Top Three Tips for Tsunami Safety

Protect yourself in earthquakes: drop, cover, and hold on.

Know your tsunami zone. In the zone, the shaking is your warning to go to high ground or inland.

Stay where you've gone. Tsunamis are tricky and can last a long time. Just when you think it's over, a larger surge may arrive.

Follow Lori Dengler Online:

Website: https://rctwg.humboldt.edu and https://kamome .humboldt.edu

Twitter: @LoriDengler

Facebook: www.facebook.com/RCTWG and www.facebook .com/kamomeboat

7

Susan Hough:
In Between the Shaking

You might find Dr. Susan Hough in her own pumpkin patch or collecting fossils with her grandson. Imagine this humble yet brilliant geophysicist traveling to countries in need—like Haiti and Myanmar—putting her expertise and compassion to work by using research to understand potential seismic hazards. Over the course of a long career in earthquake science, Sue has had a lot of firsts. While researching for her first book, she looked at the historic New Madrid, Missouri, earthquake of 1811–1812, the largest quake in the United States since European colonization of the Americas. There were no seismometers at that time, so through recorded stories of local people, she was the first to discover that the shaking was stronger in river valleys filled with sediment and to prove that remotely triggered earthquakes (quakes that can cause other quakes outside the aftershock area) can happen anywhere.

In Oklahoma, Sue was the first scientist to study the shaking of human-made, or induced, earthquakes and how they compare to natural tremblors. And later, on a diplomatic deployment to help install the country's first seismic network, she was one of the first Americans to be allowed into Myanmar, a country in political and economic strife in South Asia, as it slowly began to move toward democracy. Sue joined the US Geological Survey in 1992 as its earthquake response coordinator. She's cowritten more than 120 articles and was elected Fellow of the American Geophysical Union in 2009. She has been at the forefront of seismology ever since.

The Historic Big One

In 1811–1812 in New Madrid, Missouri, three large earthquakes (magnitudes 7.5, 7.3, and 7.5) caused damage as far away as Cincinnati, Ohio, and were felt all the way to the East Coast in Hartford, Connecticut. The shaking, 10 times bigger than that of the destructive 1906 quake in San Francisco, was felt across Arkansas and Missouri. Reports indicate there were 7 earthquakes, 200 large aftershocks, and almost 2,000 smaller ones. The shaking toppled chimneys and log cabins yet killed only one. It caused the ground to rise, fall, and crack, trees to bend, and sent landslides and flooding across the land. High waves on the Mississippi River capsized boats and washed many ashore. Along the water, banks caved and sandbars and islands washed away, with the damage extending to Illinois, Tennessee, and Kentucky. Passengers on the first steamboat on the Mississippi River woke up to find the island they'd been docked at the night before had disappeared from liquefaction, water-logged soil that lost its strength from all the shaking. To help victims of the quake rebuild, Congress passed the New Madrid Act in 1815 and offered new land to those who suffered.

The New Madrid region is still considered a high-risk area, and geologists suggest another big quake could happen within the next 50 years. Fortunately, with advanced seismic technology and scientists like Sue, large-scale damage can hopefully be prevented.

Sue's father was a professor of political science at Harvard University, and even though they weren't an outdoor kind of family, he taught her to throw a football with a pretty mean spiral. Often, they moved around the country, and the world. They also took trips together. Sue loved spending Christmas in Ridgecrest, California (ironically the site of the Ridgecrest quakes in 2019), where her grandparents lived. This idyllic location was full of desert tortoises, roadrunners, scorpions, and jackrabbits.

Sue lived in Illinois as a girl until her family moved to Toronto. There, her father encouraged her and her siblings to find adventure. They had a "long leash" and at around 8 or 10 years old, were allowed to take public transportation into the city, walk to school by themselves, and visit downtown shops and the waterfront of Lake Ontario. As the perpetual new kid, Sue considered herself shy and geeky, someone who hung out with other misfits. She loved math and writing and spent a lot of time on her own, reading or working on projects. To her, math was like a game and made sense, whereas spelling infuriated her because the rules always changed . . . and nobody bothered to tell her that in Canada they used British spelling!

In high school, she spent time with her best friend (not boy-friend) working on electronics projects, competing on the math team, and attending prom together. Sue learned basic computer programming in school and recalls several teachers of geometry and chemistry who motivated and inspired her and made the sub-jects fun. Her trigonometry teacher knew her so well that he'd save the hardest problem for her to solve in front of the class. Only four girls were in her physics class in senior year, and her teacher, an "old toad," seemed to be part of the "Old Boys Club." He didn't encourage girls to excel, which may have negatively affected her outlook on science at the time. Sue recalls that she had very few female teachers in STEM—both in high school and college. Gender norms and expectations from generations before her kept most women out of the sciences. Sue believes that with fair oppor-tunities, more female scientists would have emerged.

Before heading to college, Sue was already taking advantage of opportunities presented to her. She accompanied her dad across the ocean to live in Moscow, Russia, for a few months during the height of the Cold War. She also became an intern at the China Lake Naval Base near her grandparent's place in Ridgecrest, California. Sue performed some computer programming and worked on the F-18 jet—a fight and attack aircraft.

As an undergraduate with intentions to major in math, computer science, or astronomy, Sue attended the University of California, Berkeley. Once again, she didn't have any female professors in her STEM classes, and the lack of role models and representation gave her a sense that maybe this community was not where she belonged. By chance, she'd been looking through the course catalog and stumbled upon geophysics, which seemed to offer more of a career pathway.

Sue reflects on how women in STEM a generation before her had it worse and recalls someone telling a colleague of hers at Cal that it was a waste of taxpayer money to fund the education of a woman in science. In academia, Sue feels the glass ceiling is still in place and this "insidious bias" sometimes affects the contributions of women invited to speak at conferences, join committees, or get referenced in research papers. Sue believes more women in higher positions of power are needed to force change. Things are better; however, biases aren't entirely gone.

After earning her PhD in earth sciences from Scripps Institution of Oceanography, a part of the University of California San Diego (which she felt was ahead of its time and much more inclusive for women), Sue took on a postdoctoral scientist position at Lamont-Doherty Earth Observatory in New York. One drizzly night in 1989, Sue had been walking her dog and was ready to go inside to watch a baseball game. As she walked in the front door, her husband told her there would be no baseball tonight. A big earthquake struck the San Francisco Bay Area, and the Bay Bridge was down.

Two teams would be deployed: one to study the aftershocks and the other ground motion of the magnitude 6.9 Loma Prieta quake, which was centered in the Santa Cruz Mountains. The quake killed 67 people and caused $5 billion in damage. As a postdoctoral student in seismology, Sue assumed she'd lead one of the teams, but one of the male directors told her otherwise. But Sue knew leading this team was important and she needed to go now. So, for the first time in her career, she stood up for herself and pushed back. And it worked.

With a rented van containing over $100,000 worth of seismometers, this 28-year-old postgraduate student arrived in the field, ready to lead. But there was a large group of mostly male scientists already working on ground motion studies. Sue says they "patted her on the head" and told her to go do something else . . . in Oakland. So, that's what she did.

With her head held high, Sue placed seismometers around the once double-decked Nimitz Freeway. The upper deck had collapsed onto the lower deck, which sadly killed 42 drivers. Sue wanted to figure out why it collapsed, and what she discovered is today seismic treasure and well-known data. By mapping the near-surface geology, Sue proved that the fallen bridge coincided exactly with soft bay mud found there. Little did the male scientists who'd shooed her away know that they'd left one of the most important questions about this quake for Sue to solve. She says that being in the direct aftermath of the quake was a sobering experience and for her made earthquake hazards very real.

After joining the US Geological Survey (USGS), Sue's work in seismology began to reach communities around the world. In 2010 in Haiti, Sue led a USGS team that installed portable seismometers two months after the devastating magnitude 7.1 quake that killed 250,000 people, injured 300,000, and left 1.5 million living in makeshift camps there. She says that the humanitarian crisis in Haiti was so critical that her team had a duty as scientists to help in the face of this calamity. They worked quickly to retrieve crucial information as the immediate seismic data could lose its value over time. The data her team acquired revealed a surprise: the strongest shaking occurred not in the soft sediment like in the Loma Prieta quake, but in two places in the foothills.

Sue describes her work in Haiti as one of the most challenging and gratifying projects she ever contributed to. It was vital, she says, for her team to improve the understanding and awareness of hazards in a country where few locals ever experienced, or had been educated on how to prepare for, earthquakes such as this one. Haiti often gets dismissed by the United States, and Sue was especially touched by its level of resilience, beyond what Americans can imagine.

Working in the Southeast Asian country Myanmar has proven equally difficult. As secretary of state, Hillary Clinton began to engage with Myanmar, a nation with a past wrought with antidemocratic policy and military governments, as the country took baby steps to reengage with the world. The US government asked officials at USGS and the National Oceanic and Atmospheric Association if they'd lead a project in earthquake risk reduction in Myanmar. Sue, being her father's adventurous daughter, said yes.

Like in the Soviet Union when she visited with her father, there were very few Americans in Myanmar. Sue's work was cut out for her. She was the principal investigator, working with the United States Agency for International Development, to help develop and install Myanmar's first-ever modern seismic network. Up to that point, Myanmar still recorded its data on paper, which was very outdated. This project soon became the hardest thing she'd ever done, and the installation of the network took much longer than expected. Sue hoped to be able to use the new cellphone network that had just been activated, but it was tightly controlled by the government. Yet Sue and her team did the heavy lifting and blazed the trail, and soon other partners got involved to help move the project along. She often rejoices in how science can break cultural and political barriers.

After several trips to Myanmar working with dedicated colleagues, the network was completed in 2016. It was soon followed by the next phase—the training of experts to learn how to read the data. Yet with progress often comes setbacks. By 2019, as the project was winding down and becoming sustainable for the local community, COVID-19 and a military coup slammed the country back into chaos. Sue was reminded how science and development can be at the mercy of nature and politics.

Sue had traveled to Nepal in 2015 after the magnitude 7.8 quake struck. It killed 9,000 people and injured 22,000, sending powerful seismic waves to the capital city of Kathmandu, which fared better than the surrounding rural areas. Sue, along with international and Nepali colleagues, discovered that ancient sediments absorbed the seismic waves instead of intensifying the shaking, whereas in the mountains, landslides and severe damage occurred.

Back in the United States, Sue continues to be a voice of reason and expertise in her field. After the Ridgecrest quakes of 2019, the community looked to her for comfort. She spoke to the media and the local communities, reminding everyone of the power of unity and collaboration. "It takes a village to respond to an earthquake," Sue says, thankful that most structures in the Ridgecrest area were built after the statewide building codes of 1933. There is no way to look into a crystal ball to see what the future holds. Sue reminds us that nobody really knows if the Big One is coming anytime soon. Yet there are a few statistics that shed some light on the future of another quake hitting Southern California: there's a 65 percent chance of another magnitude 5-plus, a 10 percent chance of a magnitude 6, and a 1 percent chance of a magnitude

7. "There's a reality here we can't sugarcoat," she says. "People need to appreciate it and they need to plan."

Earthquakes are a funny business, Sue says. Their randomness can throw unpredictable curveballs in your career. So, when the earth was quiet, she stumbled into what she calls "socioseismology," or looking at how culture and socioeconomic issues affect the way people participate and volunteer in earthquake reporting. For instance, for her research, Sue is one of the leading users of the Did You Feel It app that collects information from people who felt shaking and creates maps that show the location of the quake and severity of the damage.

Sue plans to keep writing science books for the nonscience audience. She has published five books on different aspects of earthquake science and has written for several newspapers and magazines. She had the most fun writing a biography on Charles Richter, cocreator of the Richter scale, which measures the intensity of an earthquake.

Charles Richter

In 1934, American seismologist Charles Richter developed a way to measure the magnitude, or strength, of an earthquake. It's called the Richter scale. He'd been studying quakes in California and needed a way to precisely measure the force of the shaking. Using ground motion from seismometers, the Richter scale applies numbers to earthquakes via a magnitude number (e.g., M 7.1). He held a PhD in theoretical physics from the California Institute of Technology, where he later became a professor. He wrote several books, worked to improve building codes, and established a seismic consulting firm. Charles was a pioneer in seismology and helped save many lives.

Mercalli Intensity Scale

The damage from a quake in a certain location is tied to the intensity of shaking experienced in that place. This is measured using the Mercalli Intensity Scale, which describes the intensity of the quake, the level of shaking, and the typical damage that can occur.

Intensity	Shaking	Description/Damage
I	Not felt	Not felt except by a very few under especially favorable conditions.
II	Weak	Felt only by a few persons at rest, especially on upper floors of buildings.
III	Weak	Felt quite noticeably by persons indoors, especially on upper floors of buildings. Many people do not recognize it as an earthquake. Standing motor cars may rock slightly. Vibrations similar to the passing of a truck. Duration estimated.
IV	Light	Felt indoors by many, outdoors by few during the day. At night, some awakened. Dishes, windows, doors disturbed; walls make cracking sound. Sensation like heavy truck striking building. Standing motor cars rocket noticeably.

V	Moderate	Felt by nearly everyone; many awakened. Some dishes, windows broken. Unstable objects overturned. Pendulum clocks may stop.
VI	Strong	Felt by all, many frightened. Some heavy furniture moved; a few instances of fallen plaster. Damage slight.
VII	Very strong	Damage negligible in buildings of good design and construction; slight to moderate in well-built ordinary structures; considerable damage in poorly built or badly designed structures; some chimneys broken.
VIII	Severe	Damage slight in specially designed structures; considerable damage in ordinary substantial buildings with partial collapse. Damage great in poorly built structures. Fall of chimneys, factory stacks, columns, monuments, walls. Heavy furniture overturned.
IX	Violent	Damage considerable in specially designed structures; well-designed frame structures thrown out of plumb. Damage great in substantial buildings, with partial collapse. Buildings shifted off foundations.
X	Extreme	Some well-built wooden structures destroyed; most masonry and frame structures destroyed with foundations. Rails bent.

Modified from US Geological Survey

In between the shaking, Sue can be found turning her home-grown sugar pumpkins into pie, making sweet jam from her plums and loquats, or cuddling with her cat and dog. She's traveled worldwide for both research and vacation and loves visiting Yellowstone National Park in the winter in hopes of getting a glimpse of the wolves, coyotes, and eagles that call it home. Some of her fondest memories include being on safari in East Africa surrounded by giraffes and taking a balloon ride over the great wildebeest migration in the Masai Mara in Kenya. She especially loves visiting western Wisconsin where her grandsons live, exploring the natural world alongside them. And who knows, you might see her hosting the Doo Dah Parade in Los Angeles as a grand marshal with some of her seismologist sisters.

As for the future? Good question, Sue says. She keeps hoping that political stability will improve around the world, especially for the countries where she's left her seismic legacy, and a little piece of her heart. As a scientist, Sue doesn't need to know everything, but she does like knowing that there is so much more out there to figure out. If anyone can do it, it's Dr. Sue Hough.

Sue's Top Three Tips for Earthquake Safety

If a big earthquake hits, fill your bathtub with water immediately and put a good stopper in the drain. If pipes break, you won't have running water in your house, but you'll be able to use the bathtub water.

Keep shoes under your bed. After a quake, immediately put them on, so you do not step on broken glass.

Have on hand rechargeable flashlights that stay plugged in so they will have a charge even if the power goes out.

Follow Sue Hough Online:

Twitter: @SeismoSue

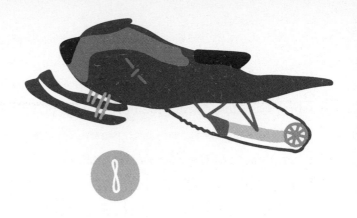

8

Marianne Karplus:
Pictures Within the Earth

Geophysicist Dr. Marianne Karplus loves remote, faraway places. As a kid, she lived all around the world—from Norway to Texas to Russia. Many powerful and talented women scientists inspired Marianne to pursue her scientific interests, including several from her own family. Besides being an assistant professor at the University of Texas at El Paso, her research includes taking pictures under the earth's surface—from the crust to the upper mantle and areas covered by rocks, water, and ice. She uses tools to measure how seismic waves either bounce off or are deflected by underground structures to better understand earthquake faults, mountains, glaciers, and heat and water systems.

She's done fieldwork in remote places like the southwestern desert of the United States and the icefields of Alaska. Trekking in freezing weather, Marianne placed seismometers on glaciers in Antarctica to record motion and icequakes, the vibrations caused from the breaking up of large masses of ice. She's used explosives to create seismic waves in Tibet and has taken images of the major earthquake fault that crosses India, Nepal, Bhutan, and other countries in the Himalayas. Why does she do it? To save lives and help people prepare for the mighty shaking below the earth. As a leader, she has seen her share of setbacks, but Marianne uses failure as fuel to make her even better at what she does. Her passion for the earth and its people shines through her accomplishments.

When she was a child, her family moved to Norway (where she learned to cross-country ski at age four), then to Texas, and then to Russia for her junior year of high school. This travel taught her how to appreciate adventure. A shy teenager, she dove into academics and especially loved her chemistry and physics classes. She struggled with confidence and felt like everyone else "had their stuff together." To cope with feeling like she didn't fit in, she journaled and penned stories, listened to the Backstreet Boys on the radio, and hung out with her two cats. During the Russian financial crisis in 1998, Marianne looked for ways to give back by volunteering at a soup kitchen and at an orphanage, where she really became aware of the suffering around the world.

The hardships of moving a lot made her stronger, yet at the same time allowed her to grow a deep appreciation for other cultures, languages, and places. As time passed, Marianne started to build friendships and open up to others. She began to realize that other people had flaws too, worried about the same things, and were not as scary as they seemed.

Marianne attended Dartmouth College in New Hampshire. There she took on more responsibilities and spent most of her time studying and learning from challenging math and science classes as well as getting her first experience doing scientific research. She double majored in math and geology. After six weeks of mapping the mountains at a geology field camp in Montana, all day, six days a week, she'd found her passion! Marianne was inspired.

Marianne's career revolves around the geophysical secrets in the earth's crust, where most of the dangerous earthquakes happen—from the thinnest crust, deep in the oceans, which can be only 2.5 miles (4 km) thick, to the thickest crust under the Himalayan Mountains, at 50 miles (80 km) thick. She wants to know how the continental crust is changing, and by studying the Himalayas in the Tibetan Plateau, it's like she's looking back in time. Fifty-five million years ago, the continent of India slammed into the continent of Eurasia and started the uplift of the Himalayas and the thickening of the crust.

Geophysics is tough stuff, but Marianne has a talent for making science more accessible. She explains this convergent process—how the two continents moved toward each other, crashed, and created the uplift of the Himalayas, like squishing a blob of clay between two wooden blocks until the clay thickens and spills out the middle. At the boundary between the two continents, or plates, is a megathrust fault, and as India continues to crash into and slip under Eurasia, a lot of stress builds that can cause a massive earthquake.

During Marianne's PhD research in crustal geophysics at Stanford University in California, she took on leadership roles and visited her field site on the Tibetan Plateau for almost two months to collect data. Building on that work, when she became a professor in 2015, she went to Nepal to collect data just six weeks after the magnitude 7.8 Gorkha earthquake that killed almost 9,000 people. Her international research team placed seismometers across the rupture zone to record information about the aftershocks to understand the fault zone. During the many aftershocks, her hotel shook, and the walls cracked. But Marianne's team didn't stop working. They gathered data that revealed the exact locations and sizes of these aftershocks, which allowed her team to map out an accurate image of the big fault that caused the quake.

In Nepal, Marianne says it was very humbling to see the destruction: the collapsed homes and buildings, people sleeping in temporary tents and shelters, and others with broken bones or injuries. Six weeks after the quake, some remote villages still hadn't received aid (food and water), and people came to their vehicles asking for help. Marianne's team did what they could by providing filters to help purify the water and giving residents rides to safe places or access to resources.

Through interpreters, Marianne listened to stories about how the local people experienced the earthquake. One of their drivers had just finished building a house for his family when the earthquake destroyed it, leaving his family to live in a small one-bedroom apartment while he worked to raise money to rebuild. It was stories like this that made Marianne realize the importance of her work, how she could help people understand earthquakes and prevent destruction.

Partnering with local scientists in Nepal, Marianne knew that her role should not be a burden on the local communities but be more of a scientific diplomat role to build partnerships with Nepalese students and researchers. By striving to see the country through the eyes of the local people, Marianne learned quickly to help them in the ways that they needed. She tried to employ local people within the project and hired some to take care of the seismic equipment. One Nepalese graduate student explained that one of the hosts she'd hired to look after the seismic station was a man from a lower caste (class) and would normally not have a way to make money.

The Nepalese Caste System

A caste is a class or group division in society based on difference of wealth, inherited rank, privilege, profession, and/or race. In 1854, the Nepalese civil code made these rules the law, and the caste system made it impossible to move up in society and promoted discrimination toward lower caste people. Even though the caste system is now illegal in Nepal, the system is still ingrained in the culture. Disasters, like the earthquake in 2015, highlight the inequalities as many of the lower-caste people lost their homes, received less health care and aid, and had fewer advocates to help them through recovery.

Working with different cultural expectations can be challenging. In many countries, Marianne says, women are told that they are too fragile to work in the field. In 2013, UNESCO (the United Nations Educational, Scientific, and Cultural Organization) reported that in South Asia, women made up the lowest number of science researchers, and Nepal had the lowest representation of all at 8 percent in 2010.

When coleading this aftershock project in 2015, Marianne worked with a talented young Nepalese woman, an undergraduate in geology. Badal Pokharel, now a PhD student at the University of New South Wales in Australia, felt honored to work with Marianne out in the field and said, "For the first time in my life, I met a woman geoscientist." As a science ambassador, Marianne is able to influence young women all over the world.

Unfortunately, gender bias exists everywhere. Wherever she is, Marianne says that both subtle and overt things can happen. Once, when traveling to small camps on the Tibetan Plateau, three Chinese graduate students insisted on accompanying Marianne to "protect [her] from the wolves" even though Marianne knew Tibetan wolves rarely attack people. Sometimes people assume that the men in a group are the leaders or the most experienced field-workers, but that is not always the case. Marianne purchases lots of tools to build equipment like solar panels, and says that often, men will assume that women do not know how to use them. But she does!

Looking back, she wished she had more experience learning how to use tools as a young girl. She acknowledges that many girls are less encouraged to build, use tools, play sports, or perform science experiments than boys are. She believes that children should be encouraged to follow their interests regardless of gender. She hopes that biases in science dwindle and the field becomes more welcoming to people of all races, genders, and backgrounds. As a project leader of her own research teams, Marianne believes in fairness and compassion, and tries to provide equal opportunities and a respectful workplace for all her students and colleagues.

Tectonic Plates

Earth's layers are classified either by their chemical composition or characteristics of rocks. The surface of the earth is broken up into seven major and eight minor tectonic plates, found under land masses and the ocean. They make up pieces of the planet's lithosphere, or outermost shell, that include the crust and upper part of the mantle.

The seven major plates are: the African, Antarctic, Eurasian, Indo-Australian, North American, Pacific, and the South American. They slowly move around on the surface of the earth. Depending on how they move, the boundaries between plates create different landforms or processes, such as valleys, geysers, mountains, volcanoes, or deep ocean trenches.

Marianne never shies away from a challenge and travels to opposite ends of the earth in order to research what's underneath it. She loves penguins and has always been drawn to remote and uninhabited snowy places that seem lonely, yet peaceful; inhospitable, yet stunningly beautiful. In 2018, Marianne joined a team of US scientists, along with colleagues in the United Kingdom, participating in a million-dollar research program that's studying the future of the massive Thwaites Glacier in Antarctica, the most unstable glacier in the region, which is being affected by climate change. By understanding the structure and dynamics of this glacier, and to improve predictions of sea level changes, they hope to collect new data to see how fast ice moves from the Antarctic ice sheet into the ocean. Using seismometers, Marianne measures seismic waves traveling through the glacier. She records icequakes to create an image of what's beneath the surface—like using an ultrasound to look into the human body. So far, Marianne's team has collected some preliminary data and hopes to be back to the edges of the earth soon to continue to help scientists predict global sea level changes.

Working in such a harsh environment can be tough, and researchers must work quickly to avoid getting harmed from exposure. Scientists work long hours through extreme temperatures (e.g., −35°F (−37.2°C) wind chill). It took Marianne a few days to figure out the right mix of clothes and hot drinks to keep her warm. She remembers on one long, frigid day, to stay warm she ran circles around the computer and sang Disney songs from the *Lion King*, *Aladdin*, and *Frozen* (of course!).

Other than Antarctica and South Asia (Nepal), Marianne has done fieldwork across the globe. Through her research, she's created models of subsurface faults and structures in recent earthquake areas that are linked to human oil and gas exploration in West Texas. She's studied the aftershocks of the 2017 magnitude 8.2 Tehuantepec earthquake off the shore of southern Mexico. In the Northern Hemisphere she has used seismic imaging and recorded seismic waves. By understanding the structure of an Alaskan glacier, she hopes to gain insight into how climate change will affect the glacier's future and its impact on Earth.

At the University of Southampton in England, Marianne used seismic imaging to understand the structure and tectonics of the Sumatra subduction zone. In 2004, a giant earthquake ruptured the greatest fault length (longer than the state of California) of any recorded quake. More than 227,000 people perished in this massive magnitude 9.1 earthquake that caused $10 billion in damage to areas in the Indian Ocean. Quakes can happen in any corner of the world, and Marianne uses her expertise and dedication to learn more about them and try to keep people safe.

Marianne's accomplishments in her field are stellar, yet she is not near done. She teaches all levels of classes, as well as takes geology and environmental studies majors out in the field for hands-on training. As a professor, she's taken students to geology field camps in the Southwest United States, to the Himalayas, and to Alaska to give them a bird's-eye view of what it's like to be a research scientist. Working in snowstorms or beautiful valleys, running to town to order pizza in a rainstorm, or sitting around the campfire on a warm spring night eating chili out of a big pot, students are inspired and get to know each other and their professor. Learning firsthand from the rocks has inspired Marianne, as well, to take even more of her students into the field to discover more about the earth and about themselves.

How Can I Get a PhD?

You might decide that you want to pursue an advanced degree, or a doctoral degree. That doesn't mean you're a medical doctor. A PhD is an academic degree focused on applying your own research to solve a complex hypothesis. You can begin working toward this advanced degree right after your first four years of college or later in your career.

In order to get a PhD, you must:

Finish your undergraduate degree with a high grade point average.

Complete a master's degree in a related or similar field of study (to your PhD).

Enroll in and complete a PhD program.

Marianne's life has taken her down many paths. As a kid, she wanted to be a sheep and goat herder and has since volunteered at a llama farm for fun. She loves running and hiking with her dogs, Willow and Chase—two rescued poodle mixes—plus playing pickup games or on teams for ultimate frisbee. Indoors, she bakes detailed cakes and pies that resemble geological landscapes found around the world, like

Iceland, the Himalayas, Tibet, and the Ethiopian Rift Valley, and has even baked an igloo cake!

Just as Marianne loves science, she loves words too. She has published poems in science poetry journals and enjoys writing fiction stories. She attends writing workshops and classes and loves using her imagination to play with words or communicate the essence of a science concept. Marianne and her friends participate in NaNoWriMo (National Novel Writing Month) in November, and both her poetry and young adult novels revolve around geological and earthquake-related themes (like the San Andreas Fault). She hopes to one day publish a novel with both exciting science and interesting characters for young readers.

Inspiration also comes from her family. Marianne's Grandma Karplus and Grandpa and Grandmom Sherman showed her through their intelligence, inquisitiveness, and thoughtfulness their commitment to science, education, and seeking truth in the world. Sharing her scientific field of study with her aunt Peggy (UC Berkeley seismologist Dr. Peggy Hellweg) has been pretty special. She admires her aunt's expertise in earthquake science, commitment to always learning more about the world, and ability to explain and teach science in such an understandable way.

Marianne has carved out her own path in earthquake science, one that has already helped unveil some mysteries of dangerous earthquakes around the world. She's not afraid to try new things, and she believes in seeking out good mentors, as well as being a mentor to others. Her motto: be somebody who listens and helps others. As we learn new things, Marianne says, it's OK to struggle and OK to fail. These are some of the best learning opportunities. Keep doing what you like to do. Eventually, Marianne believes, you will improve. "Go for it," she says. "Do what you love and care about."

Marianne's Top Three Tips for Earthquake Safety

Be prepared to take care of your family pets in case of emergency. Do you have what they need?

Think about what your family and your neighborhood might need in an earthquake, and be prepared to lend a hand.

Decide how you will communicate with your loved ones if cell phone signals and the Internet are down.

Follow Marianne Karplus Online:

Website: studyearth.wixsite.com/uteplithosphere

Instagram: @mariannekarplus

Twitter: @TeamGeophysics

Facebook: www.facebook.com/marianne.karplus

Edith Carolina Rojas: Volcano Child

You may find geologist Edith Carolina Rojas standing at the edge of rumbling volcanoes or studying remote stretches of volcanic desert. She's a professor who showers her geology students with her passion for research. She lives with a fierce determination that has enabled her to achieve her dreams that she's had since being dropped into a new country, culture, and language as an 18-year-old immigrant.

This young scientist has had her share of obstacles to overcome as a woman of color, having to work twice as hard in a White male-dominated field. Through hard work, dedication, and courage, she has earned her seat at the table and pushed against an often-biased system to help others find their place.

As a storyteller, Edith takes her students on journeys beneath the surface of the earth. With a relentless pursuit to understand how the world works, she hopes to make the world a more accessible and safer place for all. Even as a child, Edith was interested in volcanoes, and through her research, she studies both current and past volcanic activity to help us better understand how and why earthquakes happen.

Growing up in Nicaragua, surrounded by a chain of 12 volcanoes, Edith experienced the earth rumbling under her feet and ashes falling from the sky. Her childhood home sat wedged between the stratovolcano Momotombo and the cinder cone volcano Cerro Negro. On top of a hill on a dark night, five-year-old Edith watched wide eyed as lava exploded and streamed out of Cerro Negro like an arc of bright orange fireworks. People were afraid, but Edith thought it was the most beautiful thing she'd ever seen.

The world mystified Edith, and she could not stop asking questions. Why? Why? Why? Finding answers to these mysteries fed Edith's desire to understand the earth's secrets. This deep respect for nature has continued her whole life. The volcanoes of her youth remain at the heart of her passion for geology, and Edith returned to her childhood home as an adult and sandboarded down the very same volcanoes (minus the lava, of course!)

Vital Volcano and Earthquake Vocabulary

Subduction zone: an area of the earth's crust where tectonic plates meet.

Tectonic plates: massive pieces of the earth's crust that move against each other.

Stratovolcano: a volcano built from layers of lava and ash.

Cinder cone: a volcano built from lose, fragmented lava pieces that erupt and cool.

Strombolian eruption: continuous, mild eruptions with lava fragment explosions.

Seismology: the branch of science focused on earthquakes.

Seismograph/seismometer: an instrument that records the motion from an earthquake.

Edith comes from a line of strong women that she describes as "fighters, not quiet or submissive." Part tomboy and part queen bee, as a young girl she wore pants or overalls instead of dresses and didn't mind bossing boys around. Her mother believed that limits shouldn't be placed on women, which encouraged Edith to pursue a path toward science: "I never thought there was anything a woman couldn't do."

Her stepfather embraced Edith's quirkiness by allowing her to snoop under the hood of his yellow truck as he explained how an engine worked. Her electrician uncle, Tio Donald, taught her to measure voltage and understand a simple circuit. Watching him repair things fueled her desire to further understand the secrets of how things worked. Her curiosity got her in trouble too. Edith isn't proud of the time she destroyed her family's brand-new color TV in an attempt to discover the people who lived inside it.

Fascinated by what she found in and underneath the dirt, Edith dug holes in the ground and filled jars of different colored sand and soil. She conducted experiments with them in her "laboratory" in a little shed in the back of her home. Even as a scientist in the making, Edith never thought she could become one. In Nicaragua, she'd never seen any female scientists, maybe only a doctor or two. Plus, she was discouraged when teachers told her she wasn't good at math and science. For hours, and with the patience of an angel, Edith's stepdad practiced math with her on Sundays. Edith had a hard time paying attention in class. As a kinesthetic learner, she learned by doing. Sometimes her teachers thought she was misbehaving. However, Edith wanted to learn more than anything, and at home, she rewrote her notes and read extra materials to help understand the day's lessons.

At 18, Edith's hard work had paid off. She graduated high school early and started law school in Nicaragua. With some tough professors, Edith quickly learned how to be resilient, not to take shortcuts, and how to collaborate. In order for her children to get an education, her mother never had the chance to pursue a higher education. Edith understood these sacrifices and decided to never disappoint her.

However, Edith's life soon turned upside down when her mother decided to move the family to the United States. Edith was angry and felt like her life had been ripped away, even though she knew opportunities were limited in Nicaragua. Edith's mom pleaded for her to try. But trying didn't mean things would be easy.

News About Nicaragua

Located between the Pacific Ocean and the Caribbean Sea, Nicaragua is the largest country in Central America. Nicaraguans speak Spanish as well as a host of various Indigenous languages. The country is home to thousands of exotic animals like jaguars, sloths, and manatees, many of which live in protected habitats, from tropical lowlands to high mountains. For several decades, Nicaraguans have endured conflict, dictatorship, and two civil wars. Along with political and economic turmoil, the country has experienced many disasters as a result of hurricanes, earthquakes, and volcanoes. Despite poverty and unemployment, the people of Nicaragua persevere and bring much cultural and artistic richness to the world.

Living in Rosemead, California, was very different for Edith: a new language, new house, new culture, and bigger city. She recalls asking herself, *Where are the people who look like me?* She felt alone. So Edith pored over books. Rosemead had a large Asian population, but when Edith met other Latinos, many were from Mexico and sounded different than her.

Despite graduating high school in Nicaragua, Edith was thrown into adult English as a second language (ESL) classes. The local school district informed her that it would take two more years of these classes before she could earn her GED or US high school diploma. Edith didn't have two years to wait. She wanted to get her life moving, so she used her cleverness to trick the system by taking the high school entrance exam before she had taken all the necessary levels of ESL. And she scored at the top of her cohort! In addition to these classes, she took her little sister to reading circles at the library, where Edith made it her goal to watch how people moved their lips and pronounced words. In just six months, Edith learned English and was ready to start college.

Edith learned not to let setbacks stop her. Like a good scientist, she understood that if an experiment fails 100 times, you try it 101 times. She knew she wanted to apply to community college. But what would she study? After attending law school in Nicaragua, she became disillusioned about whether law was the best way for her to make a difference in the world. Edith got a part-time job to pay her tuition at Pasadena Community College, where she eventually switched from prelaw to education, a major that she felt might allow her to give back to students just like her. Edith's grandma taught her to never say no to opportunities, so even as an education major, she applied for a paid internship with the US Geological Survey—despite never taking a geology class. And she got the job! During her internship, Edith evaluated data and plotted landslides using Google Earth. Something clicked, and geology felt like home, felt like a future.

Edith transferred to California State University, Los Angeles (CSULA) and got to know all her amazing geology professors, appreciating the diversity in staff and students, which gave her a sense of belonging. Yet even with a support system, Edith lacked confidence majoring in geology. However, hands-on field research trips (in cool places like the Grand Canyon) made her feel like she was hiking inside a real-life geology book. Edith was hooked!

After graduating from CSULA and getting both her bachelor's and her master's degrees, Edith began teaching classes on natural disasters and mineralogy at her very own alma mater. Even through difficult times, like being broke and feeling lost, school became the one place where Edith felt stability. She let education be her compass, and with that compass in hand, she was able to move in the direction of her dreams.

Searching remote stretches of the Mojave Desert near Barstow, California, where geologists believed no volcanoes had ever existed, Edith's research team at CSULA wanted to prove them wrong. Under the blazing sun and with heavy gear strapped to her back, Edith grabbed a rock hammer and trekked through the desert. She observed the geology of the loose mud, sand, and soil. She broke up hundreds of rocks: some sedimentary (layers of sediment transported by water, ice, and wind) and some igneous (formed by the cooling and drying of magma or lava).

In her exploration, certain stones that seemed out of place caught her attention. Edith searched for volcanic ash, pumice, and obsidian, all by-products of past volcanic eruptions. These bits and pieces of rock, ripped from a nearby mountain, gave her hope that her hypothesis might be right. She zipped up thousands of pieces into plastic bags, recorded the location and time she found them, and tried to answer her team's big question: Was this section of the desert a volcanic center?

Pebble by pebble, her research team put together the geological and historical puzzle of this one-mile section of rock, where they noticed how the stones exhibited the same color and minerals as other volcanic rocks. Soon, Edith and her colleagues validated their hypothesis and proved that the area of her study was the site of a violent volcanic eruption long ago. It was like rewinding a piece of geological history.

Today, there are no volcanoes in the Mojave Desert, yet scientists can connect this volcanic-related seismology to earthquakes. Earthquakes and volcanoes are found on the edges of tectonic plates, and earthquakes are mainly caused by the movement of the plates. Earthquakes caused by volcanoes are generated by the movement of magma. They are called harmonic tremors because their movement and sound are rhythmic, like a song. Edith believes these tremors are beautiful, yet she knows they are also dangerous as they can take down a house. Harmonic tremors have been recorded by seismographs and help scientists better understand how earthquakes behave.

Experts use evidence of the past to predict the future. Edith believes that knowing something when nobody else does is like a treasure but says scientists have to be careful not to force the answer to their questions. The data must be accurate, and when it is, Edith says the feeling is very personal—for just a moment, a "discovery that is all mine."

Even with success, the scientific path is not always kind. In the United States, the number of female graduate students in geoscience has dropped over the last 15 years from almost 50 percent to just over 40 percent. Despite encouragement to study geology, Edith was one of a few women in the field and didn't always find herself in a friendly classroom or welcoming desert. She's had many male role models and respectful colleagues, yet Edith becomes frustrated when nobody holds those who don't treat women with respect accountable. Jennifer Garrison, Edith's only female graduate professor and advisor at CSULA, was very in tune with Edith's struggles as an immigrant and a woman of color in a man's world. Jennifer reminded her to be courageous, strong, and smart, and to push back kindly when male colleagues or professors demonstrated gender bias or discrimination.

As the only Latina in her department, Edith calls it like she sees it and will not let racist or sexist comments go unnoticed. Her credibility as a scientist has been questioned, and she has been spoken down to because of her accent. Sometimes, Edith responds in a gentle way, and sometimes she does not. Learning to push back kindly allows her to stand up for herself and for equality in the workplace.

Edith has often been made to feel undervalued in her field —not uncommon for women in academia. Nobody explained this obvious or subtle bias to her; nobody mentioned that with the lack of diverse representation in the sciences, she may experience the imposter syndrome (doubting one's abilities and feeling like one doesn't belong). Being a woman of color in the physical sciences has been tougher than she'd imagined. However, Edith has found her own family of female professors in the sciences who help lift each other up.

Edith keeps a Post-it at her desk that says, "You earned your place here. You deserve to have a voice at the table," reminding her that she's worked hard for her success. Her advice is to dedicate yourself to what you love and learn to be your own advocate. She advises others to remember that many of the insecurities you may feel are not real, that you are a gift. Edith encourages other women to follow their dreams, regardless of the obstacles. And, even when you think no one is watching, you are inspiring somebody else.

Edith believes education is the great equalizer and feels like she can be a role model to her students at the College of the Desert in Palm Desert, California, many of which share her struggles. Currently, as an assistant professor of geology on the tenure track, she teaches them about their surroundings and how to make smart decisions regarding their right to clean air and water, especially with environmental concerns at their nearby water source, the Salton Sea, and about living on the San Andreas Fault. For her English language learners, Edith uses her biliterate superpowers and tries to be the person she needed as a student. Edith believes human beings need to use critical thinking skills more than ever and pushes her students to not take anything at face value. "You must question everything you are told." Edith wants them to find answers for themselves, and she hopes they will take this tenacity to the world outside her classroom.

Ready for the Big One?

It has been a while since California has had a massive seismic event. Edith believes that the state is not prepared for one. Too many people live in buildings that have not been updated, or retrofitted, for earthquakes—many communities are not ready in any way. In California's Coachella Valley, Edith says there is only one freeway and two small highways. In a disaster situation, it would take a few weeks before help could get in or people could get out. She's fearful that even in earthquake country, people will be blindsided by a large earthquake. Edith believes that it's her duty to help prepare her students. Mother Nature will do its thing, she says. Just be ready for it and help others be ready too.

Edith feels grateful for her family, yet even with all their support, she sometimes finds herself at odds with not only them but also her culture. As a kid in Nicaragua, she didn't understand why people in her town carried statues of the Virgin Mary to the volcanoes, blessing them with holy water so they wouldn't erupt. She remembers thinking that's not how it works and went out to find her own answers. "I am a scientist to the core . . . and believe in evidence-based everything."

Culturally, her ambition and independence contradict common expectations for girls. Marriage was not her priority, and people at home thought her career choice was weird. By contrast, Edith knew from a very young age that she'd make her own rules, yet live true to herself and still be respectful to her family. She will never break her grandmother's heart, but Edith believes we all must decide what values to live by and never negotiate who we are.

Edith puts her energy into what she can control and exercise, which keeps her balanced. She strongly believes that you should follow what makes you happy and do what brings you bliss. For

Edith, one of these passions is traveling. She loves exploring places that have beautiful rock formations, such as the deserts of Utah or the big island of Hawaii. Edith's heart always takes her back to Central America, and she visits Nicaragua often.

Edith is deathly afraid of heights, which is a terrible thing for a geologist because they are often on mountaintops! But fear does not stop her. Once, when exploring Nicaragua's Masaya Volcano, she climbed to the very edge of the crater, enchanted by the beauty (and maybe the toxic gasses), and suddenly she realized that she could die. Her survival instincts took over, she says, and with a little luck and smarts, Edith made it back down safely. On an explosive 1,000-foot-tall volcano called Telica, she heard rocks crackling and felt the ground shaking from the magma under the surface. A visitor passed out from the toxic gasses, and Edith suddenly felt again how dangerous her work and passion for volcanoes is. She panicked—but for just a second. A little crackling or shaking will never hold Edith back. She tells her students, "I refuse to die a stupid death."

Every day, Edith remembers that life is too short and too fragile not to live it well. Be your best self and the rest will follow. Live it well. That's just what Edith does.

Extreme Volcano Crossing

The lure of volcanos bring more than just scientists to visit. Nik Wallenda, an American daredevil, crossed the 2,083 foot Masaya crater in Nicaragua on a tightrope. It took him half an hour to creep across while the bubbling lava and toxic fumes spewed from the lava lake below. Extreme athletes also surf down volcanoes, sometimes called ash boarding, by riding downhill on slopes covered with volcanic ash. Athletes in this sport, invented by adventurer journalist Zolton Istvan in 2002, use sandboards, with bindings, boots, and goggles. They may stand, following a slalom ski position, or sit in a luge position.

Edith's Top Three Tips for Earthquake Safety

Keep a whistle close by (her student's idea) to alert people if you are trapped or lost in the rubble.

Keep a bathtub plug handy so you can fill up your tub as a water source.

Keep extra cash in an emergency kit—credit cards, debit cards, or Apple Pay may not work.

Follow Edith Carolina Rojas Online:

Twitter: @LatinaGeologist

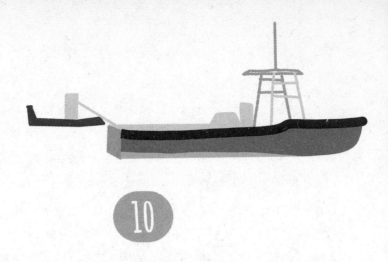

10

Valerie Sahakian: On Land and Sea

You might find geophysicist Dr. Valerie Sahakian hiking or running on a trail, or maybe surfing in the Pacific Ocean—anything that gets her outside or in the water. She worked as a researcher at the US Geological Survey and today is an assistant professor of earth sciences at the University of Oregon, Eugene. Whether using instruments to take images and characterize fault lines or measuring ground-motion and shallow earth structures to better understand past quakes, Valerie works endlessly in the field (on land and sea) to paint a clearer picture of active earthquake faults.

In hopes of finding ways to warn people, Valerie targets megathrust and tsunami-causing earthquakes like the 2010 magnitude 7.8 in the Mentawai islands, Indonesia, that took more than 400 lives. Using high-tech, seismic instruments, she's also mapped fault structure in challenging spaces underwater and in the desert. Living within the legacy of her grandfather, Alfred Abel, a trained engineman who spent a lot of time at sea, Valerie is an ocean person who adores life in the field. Yet she admits that research is mostly about trial and error and full of difficulties that require adventure, tenacity, and patience, whether encountering big storms or sharks chomping on seismometers.

As a geophysicist, she's carved out her niche in science. But as a woman, bias in the field or classroom was never far behind. She is still searching for that confidence she had as a kid but has found a support network that help gets her through. Valerie embraces failure and will never lose her curiosity that helps her solve problems in order to keep people safe during dangerous earthquakes and tsunamis.

Valerie's family is connected to the ocean. Her mother's father owned small boats, and he would take Valerie's mom out to fish or just for fun. Her granddad Alfred trained in nuclear physics in the US Navy and in 1960 was the chief engineer on the USS *Triton*, the first submarine to circumnavigate the globe. Valerie realizes how much of an inspiration her grandfather has been to her career in marine science and shares her experiences of the sea with him. She has spent many hours in the hundred acres of forest that extend to her childhood home. She remembers learning about cool science concepts like gravity from her father, who was a civil engineer. She'd ask him to read his books on bridges or engineering to her. He'd pretend-read, making complex topics accessible to her.

Growing up in Rhode Island, Valerie often traveled on ferries and made the ocean and nature part of her life. Her house butted up on a few hundred acres of forest, which she loved exploring. This became her playland, and Valerie and her friends built forts and caught frogs, looking for interesting treasures and imagining different games. One time, Valerie remembers walking far into the forest with her buddies—farther than they'd ever gone—on a great adventure. Eventually, they came across a house with people barbecuing who gave them popsicles. Lost, but never scared.

Even at school, Valerie always loved science. Each class she took sparked her interest in pursuing a career in the field. At one point she was convinced that she'd be a pediatric neurologist (she aimed high!), until eventually deciding on physics and math. Yet Valerie had to prove herself. Some of the kids in school made comments that she liked activities that "weren't for girls," like swinging on the monkey bars, jumping, or climbing high in trees. Some kids told her she was too weak or too slow. They'd make fun of her for climbing in a dress, so she started wearing shorts underneath. Valerie didn't stop. Her desire to understand nature and seek out adventure won every time, even when some older family members commented on how she should be more ladylike.

As a teenager, fighting these old-fashioned gender norms became demoralizing and affected her self-esteem. In college, Valerie recalls taking a physics class for engineers. Of the 75 students, just 5 were women. Her two lab partners, both male, would disregard her input and tell her she was wrong. Valerie ignored their negative comments, and on every test scored higher than them. In graduate school, the power dynamics between male and female professors and students were filled with inequity and double standards.

She recalls that, later as a scientist, male crew members often told her to get off the deck of the research vessels because it wasn't safe for women or made inappropriate comments. More than once, when trying to set up equipment in the field, she's been "elbowed out of the way" by male colleagues for doing it "wrong," even though she'd learned the process from an expert. How has she dealt with this mistreatment over the years? Valerie says that as a kid she was stubborn and outspoken and would tell people off, in the end doing what she wanted. However, in her teen years she withdrew, finding it harder to stay confident, which has taken a really long time for her to recover from.

Valerie thinks girls should be steadfast, confident, and believe in themselves. They shouldn't be deterred by people telling them that they're going to fail. Valerie says that failure isn't terrible and that "it's part of growth, part of life." Failure "doesn't mean anything is wrong with you." It's taken her a long time to understand that failure can be a stepping-stone to bigger and better things.

Today, bias against women in the field has lessened, but if something unfair takes place or is said, she will call it out. Over the years, Valerie has noticed that both men and women have become more willing to speak out and reaffirm gender justice. Both faculty and students in her current department are much more aware of this issue and are proactive in creating a diverse environment, willing to stand up against the wrongs of the past. She finds comfort in her support network, made up of both men and women, and it is meaningful to know that they understand the potential for discrimination.

Valerie's mother is an inspiration, as she has also faced discrimination that has affected the direction of her life. She's super creative and kind and constantly interested in new things. Her mother is especially interested in earth sciences and has a great affinity for it. She quickly comprehends things that took Valerie years to understand. Valerie thinks that maybe she's chosen this path partly because of her mother.

From her studies, upbringing, and jobs, Valerie has gathered many tools that have helped her succeed in seismology. Her mathematical intuition and strong writing skills have been vital. In graduate school, she learned how to write computer code, an ability that she sees as an absolute necessity. She worked tirelessly with other graduate students for 10 or more hours a day using a coding program called MATLAB. If it didn't run properly or had an error, it would beep. Valerie's coding beeped a lot. Her friend (and now husband) finally got tired of the beeping and offered to help. She learned so much from her peers, and that has made all the difference.

In her own research, Valerie has learned to fully embrace the scientific method, which allows her to define the validity of her science—isolating what she knows and what she needs to know. All scientists must accept that someday, someone will refute their science, changing what they thought was true. Researchers have to be OK with that, she says, and realize that science evolves. That's part of the process.

Being satisfied with not knowing the answer doesn't come easy. Valerie says that most people are used to getting the answers right and have grown up in a system where this outcome is considered success. As a scientist, one must shift perspective and understand that it is perfectly fine to get something wrong, a difficult concept to accept. What's even harder, Valerie believes, is knowing you may never figure it out. "It's not about you," she says, the science just may have not been discovered or available yet.

For Valerie, life in the field is all about real-time problem solving—figuring out how to get the best data and how to structure teamwork so that everyone has a fair and enjoyable experience. Valerie relies on her well-functioning teams as they work in tough places like the All-American Canal in the Imperial Valley in California. The All-American Canal is the largest irrigation canal in the world and has a very danger-ous current. There, they studied how local earthquake faults contributed to the slip rate, or how fast the crusts were mov-ing, or slipping, after seismic events. They hypothesized that other unknown structures or faults probably contributed to the movement. Due to human-made changes and agriculture in the El Centro/Calexico border area, Valerie's team decided to image and map the underwater structures and faults of the canal.

On two separate missions, Valerie used a massive marine seismic-reflection instrument called CHIRP (compressed high-intensity radar pulse), which was attached to her team's research boat. Her team collected sound waves that traveled through the water, sending back energy recorded from the bottom of the canal. The CHIRP was difficult to work with as it was towed off the side of the boat, which was traveling a few miles per hour. The canal had grates and stations that regulated the speed of the water, and the most grueling part of her project was having to pull the heavy equipment out of the water every time they came to a grate.

On their first trip, which she calls a pilot study, they didn't retrieve good data due to the trouble with the equipment. However, by the second outing, and with the help of Imperial Irrigation District officials who drove a boon crane truck to help support the CHIRP in the water, her team figured out a better solution to pull the equipment. Through a willingness to try and try again, Valerie and her team used the images they took to determine how breaks and separations on the canal floor could reveal new information about faults and existing structures to determine the seismic hazard of this large slip system.

As a part of her PhD program, Valerie studied the Salton Trough Fault, a fault line that runs along the eastern shore of the Salton Sea in Southern California. At an elevation of 237 feet below sea level, the Salton Sea is the state's largest inland body of water. Created when the Colorado River broke through a series of dikes and flooded the seabed, it has 130 miles of shoreline and is saltier than the ocean. Scientists believe this fault line could be thousands of years old and parallel to the infamous and treacherous San Andreas Fault.

On another project, Valerie studied data from the 2010 magnitude 7.8 Mentawai event off Sumatra that triggered a tsunami and killed more than 400 people. Shallow quakes in a subduction zone result in larger tsunamis than expected, and general warnings based only on earthquake size will predict a tsunami much too small, leading to many lost lives. Seismic data recorded across the globe can differentiate these types of earthquakes from normal subduction zone ones, but often the warnings arrive too late.

By looking closely at the geophysical data on the Mentawai event, Valerie's team found that the shaking for this quake was unbelievably low. The size of the tsunami was expected to be magnitude 8.5, not a smaller quake at magnitude 7.8. The shaking was normal for a quake with even lower magnitude, like 6.3, but the tsunami was 30 times larger than expected. Valerie's data helps researchers identify inconsistent shaking and make predictions for more accurate, and faster, early tsunami warnings that will save people.

At home in the Pacific Northwest, Valerie has plenty of projects that allow her to study seismic hazards in the Cascade Range. Like looking back in time, scientists know quite a bit about past earthquakes by looking at geology. In the Pacific Northwest, geologists like Valerie look for turbidites, specific patterns of offshore sediment layers that were formed from currents, like underwater avalanches or landslides, that they believe are caused by earthquakes. Valerie collects core samples to measure the strength of the sediment and then combines that data with physical models of fake earthquakes to see what kind of quakes could cause sediments to shake and fail. This helps her predict future outcomes.

One of Valerie's students is studying how the Willamette Valley in Oregon acts like a basin in an earthquake and shakes like a bowl of jelly when a quake hits. The seismic waves reverberate, making the quake much worse and more dangerous.

Tanya Atwater: The Mother of Plate Tectonics

Award-winning geophysics and marine geologist Dr. Tanya Atwater has spent a large part of her career at sea.

As the first to observe geophysical features along the bottom of the ocean, she created a tectonic map of the seafloor. She's worked on ships and has dived 12 times in the submersible *Alvin*, a human-occupied vehicle (HOV) that can reach depths of almost 15,000 feet. Tanya mapped the details of spreading centers, the oceanic crust formed along underwater mountain ranges.

On land, she's focused on the tectonic changes in western North America over the last 100 million years, from a subduction zone to the evolution of the plate boundary of the San Andreas Fault. Understanding how the earth's crust is broken into tectonic plates, Tanya has taught us how their constant bumping and rubbing has reshaped the earth, revealing the origins of geologic features like the Rocky Mountains, Death Valley, Yellowstone National Park, and the Cascades. She's carried the torch for women in marine science, pushing against sexist rules that prevented female scientists from conducting research at sea because of a superstition claiming they were unlucky. Tanya believes that there is no science without passion. Lucky for us, that's true.

On and offshore, Valerie has focused on two fault zones of a continuous fault system that runs across three heavily populated counties in Southern California. If those faults rupture at once, data shows that it could result in a magnitude 7.4 quake. Even though data shows that all the faults have not ruptured at once for over 11,000 years, parts of them have, including the magnitude 6.4 earthquake that hit Long Beach, California, killing 115 in 1933. Despite the difficulty of studying fault lines underwater, Valerie and her team spent more than 100 days at sea using sound waves to create images of the sedimentary layers of the ocean floor to get a much clearer picture of this fault system.

Doing research at sea can be exciting, and sometimes dangerous due to unpredictable weather. Being on ships with all kinds of scientists, Valerie says it can be fascinating to watch them troll, or fish by trailing a lure or hook from a moving boat, and often pull up strange and weird organisms like salps, a type of sea squirt, virtually transparent, barrel-shaped marine animals that move through the water using jet propulsion and link up to make chains to swim together. Once, helping with a plankton net tow, Valerie collected sea butterflies, which have jelly-like wings that help them "fly" through the water.

Being out in the middle of the ocean gives her a sense of peace. It can be exhilarating, but living on a ship with cramped quarters for long periods can be difficult. Scientists share a bathroom and a tiny cabin with one or two bunkbeds. Plus, it's tough to take a shower while the ship is moving. Valerie spends most of her time in the lab with shifts usually lasting 8 to 12 hours. Severe weather can affect the seas with high waves and wind, but with drills and training, Valerie has learned to trust the crew with her life. The longest she's been out to sea is three weeks, and luckily, growing up in Rhode Island, she's developed "sea legs."

When not working, Valerie is in the water near Scripps Beach in La Jolla, California, where she spends many hours swimming and surfing. She loves the sound of the water lapping on her surfboard, the crashing of the waves, the feeling of the spray on her skin. And having a dolphin ride the same wave is pretty cool too! She loves animals and has adopted a playful stray cat with long fur she named Huitlacoche, after a mushroom from Mexico that he sort of looks like. Her dog Sitka, a rescue puppy, is very active and when Valerie goes for a run or cross-country skis, Sitka comes along. As a runner, Valerie loves the feeling of her lungs and muscles working together and uses her passion as an opportunity to explore when she travels.

Overall, this earth scientist has been most surprised about how ideas are born. With the curiosity of a kid, she's constantly wondering about the next big question. Valerie can't wait to find answers that help reveal more data and shed light on fault lines, underwater structures, and complex processes under the earth that cause deadly quakes and tsunamis. At this point in her career, she can't wait to see where these questions take her. Her interest in science challenges her all the time, on land or sea, and Valerie would have it no other way.

Valerie's Top Three Tips for Earthquake Safety

Imagine if an earthquake hit today. Would you be able to get to your valuables quickly? What items in your home would be in danger?

What changes can you put in place to make your home safer?

For the longer term, think about community, neighborhood. What local policy exists to help prepare people? Where would your evacuation center be?

Follow Valerie Sahakian Online:

Website: pages.uoregon.edu/vjs

Instagram: @veggyval

Twitter: @terraval1

Part III
Getting Out the Word:
Seismic Outreach and
Communication

Beth Bartel: At Home on Volcanoes

Beth Bartel wants to humanize science. Whether interviewing locals around a dangerous volcano or getting frostnip on her nose while working at 11,000 feet above sea level in Antarctica, she wants to figure out how to best understand the way the earth works and communicate that science to the people who need it the most. And she works hard at it, having earned two bachelor's degrees—one in Spanish language and literature and the other in geology—plus two master's degrees, one in geophysics and one in journalism. She also is working on a PhD in geology at Michigan Technological University.

By combining her understanding of earth processes, creative problem solving, and stellar communication skills, Beth has come to understand the importance of the human element of disaster, which includes people's relationship with the science and the scientist. Beth wears many hats. She's worked as both a scientific field engineer and a data technician and as a communication and outreach scientist, focusing on the local residents, trying to understand why people live in areas with dangerous natural events like volcanoes and how they survive them. Although her experience differs between roles, Beth focuses on community: how to best collaborate with colleagues and locals to find out what both groups need and help communicate important messages for survival.

As a little girl, volcanoes, earthquakes, and tsunamis made Beth tremble with fear and excitement. She was a curious kid who didn't like to be told no and had parents who encouraged her to be adventurous. As an adult, Beth has traveled the world to study volcanoes in places like Ethiopia, the Philippines, Ecuador, Yellowstone National Park, and even in her home state of Washington. She never expected to go into science— after all, she hated math—but was lucky enough to have amazing teachers and opportunities that inspired her along the way. She's an environmentalist and got hooked on geology in college, fascinated early on with the idea of how people's ineffective responses toward natural events can turn these occurrences into disasters. This motivated her to want to work toward educating the public on how to respect and live in harmony with nature.

Beth is happiest when she has a sense of purpose. She often finds work both interesting and fun, but she lets herself get a bit wild too—whether singing "My Way" during karaoke, dancing merengue or cumbia (at home, of course), or hanging out in a big pink flamingo float at the lake with her friends. Beth appreciates living in the moment. You might find her tweeting @EatTheCrust (an homage to the subduction zone and conservation—don't waste food, and eat the crust!), doing a podcast, radio show, or making cool science videos on YouTube.

She's an author too and plans to write a book about the origin of the Cascade Mountains, which were just outside her door as a kid. But she does have her doubts, like we all do, about her abilities and place in this field. She advises others to do what makes them happy and to take risks. Failure and rejection are just a part of life and give us opportunities to grow. Beth likes to help others grow too, so watch out for this influential scientist. Whether she's doing volcano yoga for kids or trekking up an active volcano, Beth puts her heart into her science. And she gets results.

Beth remembers her second-grade teacher reading a picture book to the class about a volcano in Mexico erupting close to a farmer's field. As a little girl, she knew she had no control over dangerous natural events and had very little understanding of how the earth worked. Growing up in Seattle, Washington, Beth didn't realize that there were a couple of volcanoes nearby, like Mount Baker (currently in repose, or sleep) and Mount Rainier (geologically active), until she was in college.

As she grew older, though, Beth learned to both love and fear nature. She hiked, participated in Girl Scouts, and took every opportunity living in the Pacific Northwest to get outside—rain or shine (mostly rain). As a girl, Beth wanted to be a writer and never thought she'd go into science or math, yet she was drawn to nature. In fifth grade, she collected rocks with her friend Amy and dreamed of being a paleontologist. Science class didn't really interest her yet, but Beth loved people, and she liked the way science connected to everyday life.

Mount Rainier: Danger Just around the Corner

Beth grew up near Mount Rainier in the state of Washington. It's an active volcano. Although it hasn't had a large eruption in the past 500 years, it remains the most dangerous volcano in the Cascade Range due to its height, frequent earthquake activity, hydrothermal system, and glacier mantle. With 26 glaciers in total, Mount Rainier has more than five times as much snow and ice than the other peaks in the Cascade Range. If a volcanic eruption melted just a fraction of this ice, Rainier would send deadly mudflows into the surrounding areas. Volcanic debris flows, called lahars, can be very dangerous to people living nearby. Mudflows move like a flash flood, picking up bigger and bigger rocks and branches along the way. Over the last 10 million years, about 60 giant debris flows from Rainier have filled valleys and completely buried the surface in mud and rock.

Sometimes Beth considers herself an indecisive person. At Whitman College, part of Princeton University in New Jersey, she discovered a curiosity for the world and many different subjects. Just before classes began freshman year, someone talked her into taking the class Introduction to Geology. She remembers being completely entranced by "glorious pictures of fascinating places and processes" and learning to understand how the planet worked. Like learning a language, she found that geology had its own vocabulary—plus the field trips and the people she met were pretty cool too, so she declared geology her major by the end of the semester. She says it was love at first sight!

Beth found the photos featured in books from the natural hazards section of her school library intriguing. She was shocked by and became obsessed with images of destruction around the planet, places where the earth had torn, collapsed, or erupted from the inside out. As an environmentalist, Beth came to understand that disaster following a natural event is caused, not by nature, but by improper response and preparation by humans. Through knowledge, respect, the right resources, and action, people can learn to accept natural events out of their control and live safely in places where these environmental hazards occur. She did fieldwork in Spanish-speaking countries like Ecuador and Costa Rica. These hands-on experiences began to carve out her career path in earthquake science.

For her master's program in geophysics, Beth worked on Taal, an active volcano in the Philippines. She didn't realize the imminent dangers she faced, like lightning strikes, spewing ash, and a night in the rain with landslides gushing all around her. At times, she was really scared, but Beth said it felt amazing to be the first person to see data on her computer from GPS stations that her team installed on the volcano. Beth doesn't like things she can't see. By using tools, mainly digital, geophysics allowed her to see inside the earth, something inaccessible to the naked eye.

When she first started learning how to use GPS, there were many errors in her measurements. However, with practice, Beth began to see that the data made sense and was able to measure the small motions they were looking for. The GPS stations on the volcano showed movement outward from the main crater or inward toward it. The volcano was inflating and deflating like a balloon! Knowing she could see results from the data and could understand more about how volcanoes work, Beth realized that the information the team was gathering could help protect local people.

For over 15 years, Beth worked as a GPS field engineer for UNAVCO, a nonprofit organization of scientists and educators that manages one of the National Science Foundation's geophysical facilities. It was a dream job for Beth. She traveled the world to "middle-of-nowhere places" and got to meet lots of interesting people, learn new cultures, and eat new kinds of food. But the science was fun too, and out in the field, she took measurements on fault zones, glaciers, bogs, and volcanoes, where all the action takes place on the planet.

While doing research in Ethiopia, as part of an international team of scientists, plus two local armed guards, Beth was dropped in by helicopter to install high-precision GPS equipment that measured the team's location to within a centimeter. She and the team worked on 1,000-foot cliffs of the Afar rift, one of only two places on Earth where we can see the oceanic crust forming on land. (The other is in Iceland.) In both cases, the oceanic crust forms above the ocean because deep, hot plumes underneath feed the extra magma into the crust, pushing it upward. Beth checked out the terrain, which was full of cracks and cliffs made of dark basalt—new magma that had oozed up from the mantle to fill the cracks long, long ago. The continental crust had pulled apart so much that a new ocean basin would form if the rift continued. It was never under water, but Beth can imagine the fish and sea creatures that could exist on this landscape in the future if the rifting continues. Today, instead of sea life, you can see hyenas.

Beth lives in Washington State and uses her expertise to educate both adults and kids about some of the local volcanoes. She worked with a group of volcanologists to teach middle and high school girls about the iconic Mount Saint Helens. In 1980, a series of earthquakes (culminating in a magnitude 5.1) led to a massive eruption, bursting open this active volcano. Steam shot 6,000 feet into the air and created a 250-foot-wide crater. As the most destructive eruption in US history, the blast killed 56 people and thousands of animals, and destroyed 200 homes.

Although the volcano has awoken several times since 1980, an increasing number of people visit and live nearby, and scientists are carefully monitoring its volcanic activity.

Years later, Beth worked her magic to engage young teens in Mount Saint Helens, demonstrating an entire volcanic eruption through volcano yoga—hand and body movements that imitate the cycle and eruption of the volcanic process. Beth makes science fun, and her team even had one of the mentors, dressed in a Sasquatch costume, charge around the corner toward the teens! With a lot of screams and laughter, it was a great moment. The history of this dangerous volcano is something that the girls will never forget.

Walk on the Ocean

One of Beth's favorite places of all time is the Afar rift valley in Ethiopia, which began separating 26–29 million years ago. Beth says that there are two kinds of crust on Earth: oceanic and continental. Oceanic crust lies mostly under the sea and is unviewable. Rifts occur where the earth's tectonic plates move apart, or rift. Most are found deep in the ocean dividing long mountain ranges called mid-ocean ridges. When the plates move apart at these ridges, magma rises from the mantle to fill the gap. When the magma hits the cold sea, it hardens and becomes basalt, a new oceanic crust of dense, dark rock. But in Ethiopia, this process happens on land. Thousand-foot-high cliffs of dark basalt have formed through eruptions that then extend as the Earth pulls the crust part. With continued rifting, the tectonic plates stretch and thin, which helps to explain why there are so many earthquakes and volcanoes in northern Ethiopia. This activity gives scientists clues as to how the continents split apart. If rifting goes on long enough, the land will sink below sea level and a new ocean basin will form.

One night, when she was a field engineer working on a project in Ecuador, Beth recalls watching from a hotel miles away the Tungurahua volcano spewing hot rocks. Even at that distance, she could hear and feel the boom of each explosion. The next time Beth was in in Ecuador, she spent two months interviewing those who lived around this active volcano, wanting to understand how they felt safe enough to stay there. Working with many scientists who had built trust with local communities, Beth came to understand how important relationships are in helping to reduce risks. Compelled by the experiences of the people she met there, she began to carve out her own niche, switching gears to tell their stories in order to communicate the science. The volcano rattled more than just her nerves. It inspired her to go back to school to get another master's degree in journalism and communications.

Experts must talk to the public and humanize the science; they must learn to empathize with those living in hazardous areas. That's how things change. That's how people will stay safe. Transitioning into the role of science communication outreach specialist at UNAVCO, Beth provided information to the public that helped them feel comfortable with our restless planet. She also trained other scientists as well.

After 17 years with the organization, Beth finally decided it was time to get her PhD in geology at Michigan Technological University.

Yellowstone National Park: An Underground Hydrothermal Treasure Chest

As a field engineer, Beth installed temporary GPS systems at one of the geyser basins in Yellowstone National Park, a geological phenomenon in Wyoming. Through geological changes over the last 150 million years, the crust has been pulled apart, compressed, and eroded, forming glaciers and volcanoes and creating mountains, canyons, and plateaus. Underneath these features, we find what Beth calls a "huge plumbing system" of treasures: active volcanic and hydrothermal (water + heat) systems. Among the more than 10,000 hydrothermal features, you will find bubbling mud pots, steaming vents, and more than 500 gushing geysers. It's home to one of the biggest volcanic eruptions in the world, creating one of the largest calderas, and is the site of petrified forests from eruptions that occurred around 50 million years ago. Yellowstone, the first established national park in the United States, is like no other place in the country.

As a GPS engineer, she had to be flexible and a problem solver. If her plan A and B didn't work, she made sure to always have a plan C. The work was technical, and Beth learned a lot about power tools and construction.

As a female engineer, she's experienced gender assumptions from some men, those who presumed she didn't know how to use tools or that she wasn't in charge because she was a woman. Over the years, Beth has tried hard to balance being both a peacemaker and someone who will call out bias when she sees it. Past generations of women in science have had it much harder, she says, as certain discriminatory behaviors were more accepted and tolerated. Today, expectations are changing and moving in the right direction toward racial and gender equity—yet many people still need to catch up. Beth challenges the status quo. She's not afraid to stand up against the injustices of the world, whether they be racism or gender discrimination.

Also, Beth, her colleague and good friend, Dr. Wendy Bohon, and another partner, Adam Pascale, formed a team and started their own business called Just SciComm, incorporating change through science communication and social justice. Beth believes that getting young girls interested and having fun learning about earthquakes and volcanoes is the best way to start.

Beth loves writing just as much as science. She's currently working on a book on the Cascade Range volcanoes. Beth wants the book to help kids better understand this volcanic range, lessen fear, and inspire awe, plus get people prepared for a future eruption.

Beth needs to feel a sense of purpose in what she does. Working in geophysics and science communication gives her the opportunity to do something that is both fun and interesting, and to save lives. However, she suffers from anxiety and worries about not living up to her potential or making the right choices. Beth tries to squelch the doubt that creeps in every so often and to remember not to compare herself to others. Standing on an erupting volcano or wondering when the next lightning strike will zap across the mountain does not terrify her the most. Her biggest fear is failure.

Beth reminds herself that rejection and uncertainty are a part of life, and failure is just an opportunity to grow. She takes comfort in the fact that her life's work aligns with her passions and hopes that others carve out their own paths in this changing world. When Beth sees room for personal growth, she feels the most capable, optimistic, open, and excited. When in doubt, she always returns to her values, bringing her science mind and heart to whatever she does. Her goal? To be "fully present in this amazing world."

It seems that Beth is doing just that.

Beth's Top Three Tips for Earthquake Safety

Awareness. Are you in an earthquake-prone area, or do you plan to be in one?

Always drop, cover, and hold on, but if you can't, stay away from glass or other materials that could shatter or fall—this includes the outsides of buildings.

If you are able, have the following survival basics: a source of clean water, nonperishable food, a light source, and communications tools that do not require a power grid. These items are crucial and will allow you to help other people too!

Follow Beth Bartel Online:

Website: https://bethbartel.com

Instagram: @EatTheCrust

Twitter: @EatTheCrust

YouTube: www.youtube.com/user/bethbartel

12

Donyelle Davis: Put Your Fear Aside

Donyelle Davis always shows grace under pressure. As a US
Navy Reserve public affairs officer and US Geological Survey
(USGS) public affairs specialist, she thrives on the rush of adrenaline, whether in a disaster recovery area or a war zone. On the
front lines, Donyelle works long hours and must be quick on
her feet. She uses her background in journalism to communicate
high-profile civilian and military crisis information to the public
and other agencies. Putting her fears aside, whether communicating about a warship collision in Asia, reporting high-profile
events in Afghanistan, or providing ground support and media
coverage on the dangerous Kīlauea volcano eruption in Hawaii,
Donyelle brings her A game. As a writer, photographer, videog-
rapher, and a US naval officer, she brings not only her leadership
but also her creativity and empathy to the field.

Donyelle's journey has not always been smooth. Working her way through competitive positions in both the military and the science field has required a thick skin and perseverance. She has found much support among the strong women and colleagues surrounding her who remind her of her value and strength. As a Black woman without a traditional background in science, she's felt her share of both racial and gender bias (even from fellow female colleagues) in her supervisory roles.

Donyelle does not relent. She lives by the words of her paternal grandmother, Bernice Richardson, who Donyelle called Mama. Mama taught Donyelle that "sometimes you have to be twice as good and work twice as hard to get half as far." Growing up in Louisiana with both grandmothers by her side, Donyelle always knew she was loved. It was Mama who let her be weird and quirky. Mama supported her love of writing, drawing, and exploration, reminding her to always be strong, independent, and kind.

Donyelle was inspired by the kindness of Mama, who was one of 10 kids and had to care for her own sick mother and aunt. Donyelle's parents were very young when they had her, and unfortunately, her family life was complicated. She'd visit her birth mother, who remarried and had children with her new husband, on weekends and during the summer. Her father, who lived two doors down from Mama, remarried too, and Donyelle didn't always get along with her stepmother. Her maternal grandmother, Mommie (pronounced "My-mee"), helped guide her too. Later in life, Donyelle realized how lucky she was to be brought up with all their love. As a young girl, she felt like a bit of a mother to her siblings, saving up her own birthday and holiday money to buy her brother and sisters gifts.

Mama, though, was her absolute best friend and the one who taught her how to be independent. Together, they watched TV shows like *I Love Lucy* and old movies with actors like Clark Gable, and listened to vinyl records of jazz and gospel singers like Della Reese. Mama even hand-sewed sequined gloves and socks for her (in light of her Michael Jackson obsession) that she could wear to school.

But most of all, Mama sparked Donyelle's interest in writing and drawing, passions that helped carve out her future. Everywhere Donyelle went as a kid, she brought paper and pencil with her. She wrote as a way to escape some of the struggles and violence in her community. She created stories that allowed her to dive into fantasy worlds that stretched her imagination. Her happiest day was when Mama purchased Donyelle's first computer so that she could type her stories. In high school, her father bought her a camcorder. She began making short movies, which became another outlet for her.

Hurricane Katrina in 2005 changed everything. As Donyelle was getting ready to attend college, the destructive storm caused more than 1,800 deaths and $161 billion in damage, flooding 80 percent of New Orleans and affecting 90,000 square miles. The hurricane damaged 800,000 homes and left the most vulnerable stranded with nothing left.

Donyelle says the devastation was like nothing she'd ever seen. The suffering of the poor and the heartlessness directed toward displaced people who couldn't afford to find homes elsewhere instilled a compassion within Donyelle toward those affected by natural disasters. Her dad and stepmother opened their home to family from New Orleans after the storm, allowing them to stay for months. This experience taught Donyelle not to judge or assume things about people without knowing their stories, to remember to live with compassion and empathy, as most of us might need them eventually. This experience taught her to look at every disaster response with equity, as all people deserve safety, love, and to be given the ability to rebuild their lives.

Despite a high school counselor telling her that her ACT test scores were not high enough for college entry, Donyelle pushed forward. She couldn't afford to retake the test, but as the first in her immediate family to go to college, Donyelle was determined to let her perseverance shine. She figured out how to apply, get financial aid, and register for classes all on her own. She had learned to be independent, just like Mama had taught her. Originally planning on attending the University of New Orleans, Donyelle had to change course due to the damage the college sustained in the hurricane. Instead, she followed a friend to Louisiana Tech University.

At Louisiana Tech, she decided to major in journalism so she could tell other people's important stories. The first summer after her freshman year, an acquaintance was shot. She and friends took him to Earl K. Long Hospital in Baton Rouge, Louisiana, which served struggling African American communities. Packed with the sick and wounded, Donyelle said the hallways were like a war zone. Their friend sat around the waiting room long enough to watch two movies before he could be admitted and treated. At that moment, Donyelle knew the world needed to be made aware of the inequities she was witnessing, and from then on, she would take journalism seriously.

After earning her master's degree in mass communications at Louisiana State University in 2012, Donyelle took a job as a multimedia journalist at a newspaper in Rochester, New York, called the *Democrat and Chronicle*. She reported on local issues, breaking news, and in-depth investigations, and she directed and produced photos and videos for social media platforms. All the while, Donyelle had applied twice to become a public affairs officer with the US Navy Reserve, a competitive position. In 2007, Donyelle joined the US Navy Reserve in hopes of becoming a journalist. Since the job wasn't available at that time, she became a master-at-arms, or military police.

Donyelle's commanding officer at the Navy Operational Support Center believed in her potential and offered to send her to Italy for six months as a mass communications specialist to help make her status more competitive. Since she'd never worked in communications for the navy, Donyelle used her civilian skills to figure out the job. Not everyone she dealt with felt she was qualified, but Donyelle worked hard, picked up extra assignments, and proved her value. She found much success on her tour in Italy, even though she was not selected yet a third time for the job as public affairs officer.

Another commanding officer noticed Donyelle's talents and offered her a mass communications specialist job and a chance to go on active duty in Manama, the capital of the Middle Eastern country Bahrain. She accepted and soon heard that she was also a finalist for a position that she had applied for at the USGS. While still in Bahrain, she did her first round of interviews for the USGS job. She was dead set on leaving the harsh East Coast weather of Rochester behind and moving to sunny California. The newspaper she worked for in New York was going through a transition, and all its employees needed to reapply for their jobs. Donyelle did not reapply. She stayed positive and wanted the USGS position more than anything.

Unfortunately, she didn't get the job, but a phone call from USGS soon after brought good news. They wanted to interview her for a new position with a unique group called Science Application for Risk Reduction (SAFRR.) This position entailed working with three different agencies that dealt with communications, early warning, and emergency risk management. In this role, she could put her unique skill set—writing, video and filmmaking, implementing new ideas, and the ability to work under pressure—to work. Justin Pressfield, her first boss at the Office of Communications and Publishing, and Dr. Lucy Jones, who led the Science Application for Risk Reduction group, both welcomed her and became her fiercest supporters. Donyelle respected them as they themselves contributed new perspectives to the field and challenged its norms.

However, some scientists believed that Donyelle's job got in their way, and as experts, they did not need to be trained or taught how to communicate their research. Donyelle didn't have a science background or a PhD, plus she was a 20-something and the only Black woman in the office. Donyelle believed that she was not valued as she should have been, and she was also often mistaken for a secretary or intern. Yet even though the other scientists pushed back, Dr. Lucy Jones took her under her wing and taught Donyelle everything she needed to know. She valued Donyelle's ideas on how to improve earthquake response and early warning plans. And through her perseverance (and working twice as hard, as Mama taught her), she finally heard that her public affairs officer package was accepted by the US Navy Reserve. She was now a public affairs communicator for both a civilian and a military organization!

In both positions, Donyelle "lived off adrenaline." She thrived working long hours that required quick, on-your-feet strategizing. Early on, while training in Japan, the USS *John S. McCain*, a US Navy warship, collided with a Liberian-flagged tanker. As part of a team, Donyelle worked 15-hour days responding to the event, first countering false information that included who was involved and the number of people killed. She learned so much about the work and herself.

With each disaster that Donyelle had to communicate information about, she gained more insight and came to understand four important things about her work:

1. Take care of your team.
2. The less sleep you get, the more mistakes you make.
3. Show grace. People are stressed and exhausted, so don't take anything personally.
4. Make your decisions when the time comes and don't question them.

Donyelle had to fill many roles all at once, and continued to make decisions. People took notice. Still operating as a Navy Reserve public affairs officer, her work with Resolute Support, a NATO (North Atlantic Treaty Organization)-led mission to train, advise, and assist the Afghan National Defense and Security Forces, sent her to work in Afghanistan from 2018 to 2019. She worked as the only US Navy member on an international team tasked with producing communications and content for both print and online media. Working close to the front lines, she grew close to her Romanian, Polish, and Italian counterparts. With every explosion and nearby attacks, they became closer: "I trusted them and they trusted me," she says. From her perspective as an African American woman in a supervisory role, conflicts arose, and this international group of coworkers and friends supported her through and through—and she still remains closely connected to them today.

While at the USGS as a public affairs specialist, Donyelle worked on a short detail as a congressional liaison, where she kept up communications between Congress and the workings of the USGS. In this position, she experienced one of the most impactful projects yet. Donyelle describes working on the Kīlauea eruption in Hilo, Hawaii, in 2018, as an intense experience. It destroyed 600 homes and left 2,500 homeless. She provided boots-on-the-ground support for about two weeks, although working a response of this magnitude was intimidating. Donyelle was determined to figure it out and communicate the information she gathered in order to save lives. At first, she hosted daily teleconferences from the USGS Hawaii Volcano Observatory, a clifftop facility right on the rim of the crater. "You could literally walk out and see the caldera smoking," Donyelle says. However, it became too dangerous to stay. From a new operations point at the local university, Donyelle managed the daily media operations and set the battle rhythm every day. She also hosted press conferences and created daily update videos. By far, the best part was working with an amazing group of female volcanologists who made her feel a part of the team.

Kīlauea's Lava Lakes

As the lava surface rises, it may ooze around the edges of the crater at Kīlauea, creating a dark and dangerous lava lake. Over the last two centuries, the crater filled and drained many times. Once, a hundred years ago, the lava rose slowly until the deep crater was so full of bubbling lava that it spilled over the rim. Within a year, the rising stopped abruptly and the lava surface dropped in just one morning, leaving just a tiny lava lake at the bottom of the crater. After an eruption in 1959, there were 17 spectacular lava fountains, filling the crater halfway with the bubbling red liquid. Volcanic activity is a continually changing process, and scientists watch how Kīlauea, this volcanic beast, may continually fill or empty its crater. Just one rule for these lakes, though, "No fishing! No swimming!"

Ironically, Donyelle felt her first earthquake in Hawaii (due to volcanic activity) while staying near the observatory. She said it felt like an elephant ramming the side of her cabin. Waking her from sleep, she dropped to the ground thinking it was a military attack! But her scariest and most exhilarating moments were while taking volcano overflights to collect video footage. Afraid of heights, Donyelle wasn't sure she could do it. She called one of her mentors, Dr. Kate Scharer, who reminded her that this was a once-in-a-lifetime experience and to put fear aside and make things happen. Donyelle was petrified in the tiny helo-aircraft that felt as small as a drone. As they flew toward the fissures, she closed her eyes, but then—slowly—opened them. The erupting volcano before her was the most magnificent scene she had ever seen. Donyelle says she could have never imagined, even in her wildest dreams, something as breathtaking. She began recording, and immersed in the experience, her fear disappeared. Donyelle made a deal with herself that moment. She would never again let fear impede an experience.

Another one of her most valuable experiences was working on the response to the magnitude 6.4 quake that rocked Puerto Rico in 2020, killing one person and causing massive damage to the southwest coast of the island. She briefed congressional members on what was needed in the response and ways to help. On the ground, Donyelle worked with other amazing women from the USGS, like Dr. Sara McBride and Lindsay Davis, to educate the public on the aftershocks.

Through all of her projects, Donyelle weaves in one common thread—importance of people and community. Over the years, she's brought humanity to the forefront of her videos, photography, and articles by documenting the forgotten and the overlooked, such as a homeless community in Rochester, New York, and the inescapable effects of addiction, or by telling the true, heart-wrenching stories of the guides and sharecroppers along the tourist attractions on Louisiana's River Road. Through her work, she's been able to honor her mentors and bring equity, compassion, and humanity to her subjects.

Inspired by Dr. Jinx Broussard

An award-winning professor, scholar, author, and public relations professional, Dr. Jinx Broussard teaches public relations, communications, and media theory and history at Louisiana State University (LSU). Recognized for her innovative teaching and mentoring of students and faculty, her leadership in education shines. Her research focuses on the Black press, racial and ethnic minority representation, crisis communication, and the civil rights movement, just to name a few.

For Donyelle, Dr. Broussard has been not only a mentor but also an inspiration. For Donyelle's master's thesis at LSU, she got permission to create a documentary titled "The Untold Stories of the Great River Road," a project that highlighted the lack of accurate representation of slavery and contributions of Africans and African Americans on the massive sugar plantations along Louisiana's River Road, one of the state's most profitable regions pre–Civil War. Lined with the iconic Southern-style plantations, the 70-mile Great Mississippi River Road follows the river between Baton Rouge and New Orleans. Its economic and cultural prominence eventually declined due to destruction from the Civil War and weather, and as of today, only a dozen plantations are currently open to the public as a tourist attraction. Donyelle's documentary helps to promote the untold stories of the Africans and African Americans who lived and worked on these plantations, the people who fueled this economic success despite enduring the horrors of the institution of slavery.

Sitting on Donyelle's graduate committee, Dr. Broussard was one of the first Black students to attend the journalism department at LSU and the daughter of sharecroppers. Dr. Reginald Owens, the head of journalism at Louisiana Tech, Donyelle's undergrad program, and also one of the first Black graduates of Louisiana Tech, had encouraged Donyelle to go to grad school and was a big part of how she explored the idea of telling the true and dark history of these tourist attractions. Donyelle was honored to present "The Untold Stories of the Great River Road" project as her master's thesis—to tell the true story of racial and social oppression of the sharecroppers who lived on the sugar plantations in this region of the state.

When Donyelle is not risking her life in the field, you might find her playing video games like *Assassin's Creed* or rocking out to a 1980s Stevie Nicks song like "Edge of Seventeen." Mama taught her to go out into the world and live it to the fullest. That's just what Donyelle has done.

Donyelle's Mama made her feel like she could do anything. She doesn't deny how her experience as a young Black woman with a traditional background has led some people in her field to believe she didn't deserve a seat at the table. Yet Mama's words always circle back, and Donyelle's proven her wisdom, value, and dedication time and time again. She hopes someday to lead a large, multifaceted science communications project and wants young women heading into science communications to believe in their skills and talents.

If she could, Donyelle would tell her younger self to "never be discouraged by doubters," no matter what. You can, she says, and *will* achieve everything you put your heart into. Donyelle's heart is invested in bringing important life-saving messages to people through powerful words and images. And with this passion she not only inspires others to take action but also reminds us all of the power of our dreams.

Donyelle's Top Three Tips for Communicating Important Messages

Know your audience and meet them at their knowledge level.
Build partnerships.
Keep your message simple, understandable, and visual.

Follow Donyelle Davis online:

Website: www.DonyelleDavis.com

Twitter: @DonyelleDavis

Kate Gonzalez Long:
Telling the Story of Science

In her first career, Kate Gonzalez Long was a bohemian artist who helped make music videos with contemporary rock and pop bands and performed political street theater. Who knew she would later become a renowned expert in earthquake response?

Kate developed essential skills from various influences in her childhood. She struggled with dyslexia and believed that she wasn't smart. Her mother instilled in her a love for books, even though reading them was difficult. Writing was also a struggle, but luckily, Kate attended an experimental high school where she could use verbal skills in class instead of writing. Kate was adopted, and she developed pretty keen research skills searching for her birth parents. The influence of the anti-Vietnam War era led her to become a political activist. Kate knew that she wanted to make a difference in the world.

As a teen, Kate balked against society's traditional norms for girls regarding their career aspirations in traditionally male-dominated academic fields. Kate's identity evolved during the women's liberation movement of the late 1960s, and she happily rode the second wave of feminism into the 1970s.

Having worked her way up to the role of line producer in the film industry, Kate learned how to manage just about everything. Yet she still longed for more. On January 17, 1994, the earth began to shake as a magnitude 6.7 earthquake hit Northridge, California, which caused more than 50 deaths and 9,000 injures and left more than 125,000 people without homes. The event inspired Kate to help make a difference in the recovery by volunteering at her local city council office, which led her to help organize the rescue response.

Before she knew it, she was hired by FEMA, the Federal Emergency Management Agency, where she worked for two decades in emergency management. Currently, she's the earthquake program officer for the Dr. Lucy Jones Center for Science and Society. Before that, Kate was the earthquake program officer for the State of California and worked for the city mayor's office in Los Angeles. As a social scientist, her adaptability, stamina, and leadership in bringing people together make Kate a trailblazer in seismic and disaster hazard and communications.

Kate was raised to believe that she could change the world. She's found an amazing support network of fierce women in her field. To educate the public and reduce the impact of future quakes, she searches out colleagues who are willing to think outside the box and who love what they do. These relationships are what Kate calls "currency." Her primary aim is to empower people to prepare before a quake and take action that might save lives. By working in emergency management, Kate has learned that life can change quickly, which reminds her to be grateful for every moment.

In third grade, Kate believed that boys were stronger than girls but that girls were smarter. She remembers asking her mother why there had never been a female president. Even though her mom fit the traditional societal norms of the 1950s and rarely created a stir, she taught Kate that she could do anything. Yet school was tough for someone with a learning disability. Kate didn't find out until college that she was dyslexic. As a younger student, she had difficulties spelling, reading, writing, and in math because letters and numbers looked jumbled. Little was known then about learning disabilities, and her sixth-grade teacher told her that she'd never graduate from high school. But that didn't stop her. Kate says that dyslexics are really good at work-arounds, or alternate ways to complete a task, master a skill, or solve a problem. She did whatever it took to learn. Extremely curious, Kate often tried to figure out what the world wanted from her and assumed that "everyone got that manual," except her.

She does not remember being encouraged to take an interest in science or subjects that required her to ask questions, develop theories, or do experiments until she landed in an experimental high school in Southern California, which operated on a college-like schedule and taught students to think critically and to defend their thoughts. Kate adapted and found ways to make learning more accessible, like reading aloud so she could hear the words. Her ability to vocalize what she read led to her interest in performance art and poetry, which earned her As and Bs instead of Cs, like at her old school. No one at this high school knew about her previous struggles. So, she started fresh. She read her way through all the classics, books written by the likes of William Faulkner and Ernest Hemmingway.

During her first year at this new high school, a group of popular girls gave her bad advice. They told Kate that if she "used big words, no boys are going to like you." Even with this poor guidance, she was flattered that they'd noticed her, as she just wanted to finally have friends. Kate believed them and joined their group. She started acting differently—reading less and doing poorly on her homework just so she could ask boys for help. But that all changed at a lecture in world history class when one of the girls at her school gave a talk on women's liberation and discussed topics such as equal pay for equal work. Kate had never heard of feminism before. After the talk, the presenter gave her a copy of Robin Morgan's *Sisterhood Is*

Powerful, a feminist manifesto and anthology of essays and historical documents on women's struggles and rights.

A Book That Changed My Life

Many minds were blown after reading the often-banned book *Sisterhood Is Powerful*, edited by Robin Morgan, in 1970. It's considered the first collection of writings from the second wave of feminism. Feminist ideas from this bestselling text spread like wildfire and inspired debates and marches, new laws, and academic fields of study. Considered the book that started the modern women's movement, it's more than just a collection of feminist-inspired articles and essays, it discusses systemic gender issues and modern feminism in terms of race, family structure, sexual reproduction, and politics. This book changed Kate's life.

During Kate's teen years, the outside world had erupted into political unrest with the anti–Vietnam War, women's rights, and the civil rights movements. Kate says that it was an iconic time to be an economics and political science major at Mills College, an all-women college in the San Francisco Bay area. Still needing to find the right answers, Kate didn't feel powerful as a learner. Looking back, she wishes that she could have been more of an advocate for herself and her own needs in school. Yet Kate wove the politics of the time into political performance art, and after graduation became part of a street theater company that focused on political issues. She made money as a cocktail server, married a musician, and lived in a commune with her theater company—and could never imagine working a nine-to-five job.

However, life doesn't always go as expected. Eventually, Kate began working in the movie industry. At first, she worked as a line producer, a manger of sorts who works on physical production with the writer and director, focusing on the script, costs, sets, and crew. Kate learned to make herself indispensable and that there was no such thing as saying no. She says that if someone asked you to put an elephant on the Eiffel Tower, you wouldn't say, "That's impossible"; you would ask, "What kind of elephant?" She worked on rock videos for Japanese bands and on the filming of the iconic band U2's "Where the Streets Have No Name" video, a completely unpermitted performance on a rooftop in Los Angeles. Kate became an associate producer on several big movies, but in her heart she wanted to do something for the "impact of the public good."

The 1994 Northridge quake in Southern California changed the direction of her life and gave her the chance to make a difference. That day, she had an interview scheduled with Universal Pictures for a production executive position, but the quake derailed her plans. It caused power outages in the region and Kate felt useless, so she headed to the local city council office to offer her help. In the midst of the chaos, phones were ringing off the hook with people asking if their buildings were safe. Kate gathered their information and organized the data in spreadsheets, working with engineers and building inspectors to help keep people safe and informed during the response. She says, "You see a hole and you fill it." That's emergency management.

A few weeks after the quake, leaders at FEMA (the Federal Emergency Management Agency) took notice of her skills and hired her as an outreach worker, for about three to four months, to gather intel from the general public about damages caused by the quake. Kate worked in FEMA's temporary office at a card table. Daily reports collected by outreach workers piled on her desk, and she was tasked with making sense of all the information. With her self-taught, analytical mind, she crunched the data and labeled reports "unresolved" if a victim of the quake hadn't received the help they needed. Even without any formal training, she took it upon herself to make sure that these people were getting assistance. For two months, she worked ten-hour shifts, six to seven days a week, which didn't faze her; Kate was used to working nonstop from sunup to sundown in the movie business.

Her commitment was obvious, and Kate's career took off. The first job in her new career was as the plans chief for the California Governor's Office of Emergency Services (Cal OES), and later she was promoted to program manager, where she worked on long-term recovery efforts. Kate continued to soar, taking a political appointment for the office of the mayor of Los Angeles in community earthquake readiness. She returned to FEMA on a national response team and also worked for the California Science Center in Los Angeles.

In 2007, she returned to Cal OES as the earthquake program officer, where she was sent to work with the US Geological Survey (USGS) at the California Institute of Technology. There, her goal was to make sure earthquake data was translated into policies and programs that changed public safety by ensuring emergency managers understood the science and used it to act in split-second decisions. Working closely with social scientists, Kate aimed to make people want to act. Basically, she became a super-hero—someone who took scientific ideas and helped emergency workers understand them in order to save others during disasters.

Kate worked on the Great Southern California ShakeOut scenario in 2008, a large-scale practice drill created to educate the public about earthquake preparedness. Led by Dr. Lucy Jones, a diverse group of experts—earth scientists, engineers, and economists—came together and created a public drill that painted a picture to simulate effects in the event of the Big One. Though Kate was not an author, she was one of the principal leaders of the first public drill. Using social science principles, Kate helped develop ideas that would change people's behavior before, during, and after an earthquake . . . without scaring them.

Just as in the movie business, Kate remembers how everybody chipped in and took a chance on this outside-the-box creative project. The first official earthquake drill occurred in 2008 and included 5.4 million participants, spanning eight counties in the state.

The program has since soared, and along with her colleague, Mark Benthien from the Southern California Earthquake Center (SCEC), Kate was instrumental in the Great ShakeOut becoming an annual and global event. By 2019, over 21 million people across the United States and 60 million worldwide had taken part in the Great ShakeOut! In addition, Kate has been influential in developing the Earthquake Country Alliance, a networking group that promotes shared social science and physical science–based preparedness messaging year-round. The Great ShakeOut allows Kate to connect her colleagues— Dr. Dennis Mileti (former Natural Hazards Center director) and Dr. Michele Wood (California State University, Fullerton community health sciences professor)—and put their preparedness communication principles into practice.

Dennis Mileti: World-Renowned Master of Disaster Communication

Kate credits Dennis Mileti, the former head of the Natural Hazards Center in Boulder, Colorado, as one of her biggest mentors and supporters. With his expertise in earthquake education and disaster communication, Dennis studied how humans accept information about alerts and warnings. Kate says that he encouraged and respected social scientists (like her) who worked with physical scientists in the last mile, where the science gets turned into policy and people change their behavior —where lives can be saved, or lost.

Dennis's research on how people perceive disaster communication was instrumental in the development of the ShakeOut scenario. Kate says his contributions far exceeded his research. He brought joy and curiosity to his work and all those who worked alongside him. Kate says he was a one-of-a kind mentor and friend. Dennis passed away from COVID-19 complications in January 2021 and will be forever missed.

Stationed at USGS at the California Institute of Technology as the state earthquake program officer for Cal OES, Kate understands how to speak like a scientist even though she didn't follow the traditional path into science. It was up to the scientists to communicate their ideas clearly, and Kate let them know that if she didn't understand their message, neither would the government and local decision makers. In an institution full of scientists, they called her the implementer, and treated her nicely. When she began working in this role, she had to take a lot of notes and then run back to her office and look things up online after meetings were over. But the most important thing she learned was to admit when she didn't understand something. Eventually, Kate realized she should not be afraid to dive into something new and ask questions.

Kate has collaborated with different authorities in the field of disaster and emergency management. Together, through multiple perspectives, researchers are able to synthesize the science so that it can reach a broader range of people, communicating ideas that could help reduce the impact of a seismic disaster and save lives. Her job was to teach people to listen to information in a critical way—to create a culture where critical thinking was a part of everyday life. Kate believes that it is important to teach people how to understand and find reliable news, and once people understand earthquake science, they are more likely to feel empowered and do something about preparing for the next event.

As a woman, Kate's long and unique road into the sciences has not always been free of conflict. Life in the movie business could be tough for women on set several decades ago—and still is today. While Kate was a young woman in the business, there was no human resources department to provide support or guidelines, very few females were in positions of power, and women had to live with harassment. Kate often found herself in uncomfortable situations where inappropriate jokes were made. It infuriated her, but bringing attention to these occurrences would damage her career.

After moving into emergency management, working for the government provided a much safer environment with stricter rules about discrimination and equity. While men mostly held higher positions, affirmative action opened doors for women in middle-management. Yet Kate recalls times early on when she was patted on the shoulder by her older male colleagues and "treated like a small furry animal or child." The culture was male-dominated, and sexism resulted.

Times have changed, and at the USGS, Kate has found tons of female seismologists who support each other. But systemic issues that promote gender bias are still at large. Kate recalls the tale of two fish in which one asks the other, "How's the water?" and the other answers, "What water?" That's how sexism works, Kate says. It so pervasive, you don't even know you're in it.

Kate often has had her doubts about her own career. She's a journeyman, someone who has learned her science in emergency management by doing, not necessarily from a career in academics. At times she feels that she's "not a scientist, but I play one at work." But as her colleagues remind her, she is an expert in her field. Because of her natural leadership abilities, innate analytical mind, and her talent at bringing scientists of all disciplines together, Kate has made a difference in preparing people for earthquake disasters over and over again.

If she could talk to her younger self, Kate would say to not to be afraid to ask questions and always be curious. Nowadays, she's found that being old is way cooler and more awesome than she ever expected. She dives into all her interests. As a creative writer, Kate writes micro-fiction, essays, and poetry. She belongs to the L.A. Poet's and Writer's Collective, where she is currently editing an anthology called *Side-Eye on the Apocalypse.* She loves the work of poets Naomi Shihab Nye, a previous Young People's Poet Laureate, and the famous Amada Gorman.

With gratitude, Kate says that her work in earthquake emergency management has truly fulfilled her. It was a quake that helped her find what she was searching for, and all the hours and sacrifice she's put in over the course of the last two decades have helped her to further the human condition. By communicating the science and getting it into the right hands, we can take care of each other.

Kate's Top Three Tips for Earthquake Safety

Water. Period.

Keep a pair of shoes tied to the leg of your bed. In one, put an extra set of your keys, and put a flashlight in the other. And if you wear glasses, keep an extra pair in the shoe as well.

Refill your gas tank when it's half full, and meet your neighbors now!

Sara McBride: Humor and Heart in Emergency Response

Dr. Sara McBride is a social scientist and expert in crisis management and response. She has researched and worked on projects in risk reduction, education, science communication, and humanitarian response in places like Namibia, Samoa, Fiji, and the Solomon Islands. However, much of her career, and her heart, is found in her second home—New Zealand. Her current position, social science coordinator for ShakeAlert at the US Geological Survey (USGS), has taken her back to the United States to Santa Clara, California, where she continues to combine her expertise, compassion, humor, and innovation to connect and save lives.

Throughout several decades of working in disaster relief, Sara speaks the language and culture of people in need, whether explaining earthquake science to regular folks or learning to speak pidgin in the Solomon Islands. With her big heart, understanding of culture, and down-to-earth sensibilities, Sara connects to those who have suffered in a disaster. She's a dedicated communication researcher and social scientist who will sleep under her desk for days on end to help save lives. And whether it's surviving on cake, funny memes, or plain adrenaline, Sara gets the job done.

After a long and successful career in communication, Sara decided to return to school to earn her PhD in English and media studies, fostering a mix of many disciplines. She had to learn to embrace failure and ask for help while working on her PhD. Sara embraces her femininity, and you might find her wearing a kimono, long, dangling earrings, and bright red lipstick. But she's faced gender bias for being too feminine in her field of science. Inspired by other women, Sara perseveres, embraces change, and remembers what she was meant to do: tackle earthquakes and tsunamis, learn to communicate how they work, and empower people to deal with disasters.

Sara grew up on a three-acre farm in the high desert area near a nuclear production site in Eastern Washington. Her father, a nuclear chemist, beekeeper, and real cowboy from Utah, met Sara's mother there, a nurse practitioner who was born and raised in France. According to her father, Sara was profoundly female as a little girl. She would cry if her parents made her wear pants or colors other than pink. Sara even snuck dresses under her ski clothes! But this never kept her from getting dirty and being curious about the world. During the summer, she helped her father uncap beehives and scrape out the buckwheat and watermelon honey from them. She loved to fish too, mainly because her two older brothers didn't like to clean the fish (she didn't mind!).

In high school, Sara fell in love with writing, literature, humanities, social science, and math. Unfortunately, when she volunteered to solve a math problem in a new way in front of her class, her teacher made fun of her. Instead of validating her work, the teacher made her feel bad about herself, even though she had the second highest math aptitude scores in the county. She began to hate math, angry at herself for letting this teacher "determine her relationship to a topic she loved."

After getting her bachelor's degree in law and justice at Central Washington University and completing a year of law school, Sara wanted a change. At 23, and with enough money to travel for a year, she flew from Los Angeles to Australia to work for Sydney BBC when the tragic events of 9/11 happened. She landed in New Zealand, unaware of this horrible attack, and came face-to-face with TV cameras and crews—plus a lot of tears. Airports shut down worldwide. With her country in turmoil and her plans to fly to Australia derailed, she stayed and worked at the New Zealand Blood Service for several years. But the tragic events of 9/11 inspired her to learn more about disaster work, so she returned to the United States to attend graduate school for public administration and disaster management from 2003 to 2005.

After earning a master's degree from the University of Hawai'i, she returned to New Zealand in 2005. Sara was hired by the Canterbury Civil Defence Emergency Management Group in Christchurch, where she immediately put to work her empathy, patience, resilience, and risk- and disaster-management skills.

In 2009, as the public education and public information coordinator, her first large disaster response came after an magnitude 8.1 earthquake struck between Samoa, Tonga, and American Samoa. The massive event generated tsunami waves of up to 72 feet high, killing at least 192 people in Samoa and ravaging the islands with over $200 million of damage, destroying and sweeping cars, houses, and buildings out to sea. Sara witnessed the devastation: entire villages washed away, gigantic container ships lying on their sides, and too many caskets—especially burials for small children who could not run away from the tsunami. She recalls meeting an older woman who was sitting under a tarp—a survivor whose grief was so severe she couldn't speak because she had had to choose which two of her four children to save. The grief and destruction were overwhelming and still stick with Sara today.

Despite tough working conditions and being surrounded by tragedy, Sara knew this was what she was meant to do. Disaster work also made her realize that "life was too short to live miserably."

In 2010, Sara worked for World Vision, an international organization that aims to alleviate poverty by helping children, refugees, and victims of disaster access education, clean water, and other necessary resources as well as supporting job and economic opportunities. She spent a year in the Solomon Islands east of Papua New Guinea as the advocacy and human relations advisor, building outreach and improving disaster communication. On these islands, there's a juxtaposition of beauty and suffering: you may find beautiful, white sandy beaches (where she learned to scuba dive) or a desperate family of 30 with one T-shirt to share between them. This diverse society has the third highest infant mortality rate in the world and is one of the poorest countries, hit hard by food, fuel, and financial crises and civil war.

The locals, mostly Melanesians, have been living with the same traditional cultural values for tens of thousands of years. Across the islands, 128 languages are spoken. The term *wontak* translates to "I will look after you because you speak the same language." It refers to the close bonds and kinship between the small groups found throughout the islands. To engage on a human level, Sara learned to speak Solomon pidgin—a mix of English, Melanesian, French, German, and Spanish—an old, universal language that connected all Solomon islanders. In some villages, seeing a Caucasian woman was uncommon. One little girl touched her arm, and when Sara responded in pidgin the girl looked to her mother and said, "I think she's just like us." The young girl then took Sara to see her garden and meet her grandmother. Sara made a connection, and language changed everything.

Strict gender rules extend throughout the islands, so Sara learned quickly how to follow appropriate norms. The beach was divided into male and female sections. She wore a loose skirt over her board shorts to cover her legs and made sure to have a local friend or guide escort her when she needed to go out. With no cell service, outside communication, indoor plumbing, electricity, or toilets, Sara learned to rough it.

Sara adapted and drank kava kava, which is made from a spicy root that tastes a bit "like dishwater." She dined on the foods that the locals ate, such as fish wrapped in banana leaves and covered in coconut milk and veggies, like sweet potatoes and slipper cabbage (a cousin of okra), a superfood that has sort of a slimy membrane. These foods helped connect her to the culture and the people, and she was often spellbound by the bravery and tenacity of those she met. For instance, she met the head of education in the Makira Province in the Solomon Islands, who had been a victim of child trafficking and escaped her fate, taking a backpack and two of her children to board a ferry to a new life. Sara could have been happy living in the Solomons her whole life, but New Zealand called again in 2011—this time in the form of a magnitude 6.3 earthquake in the town of Christchurch that killed 185 and injured thousands.

Returning as the public information manager, second in command, Sara was in charge of initiating the emergency text message system, holding community briefings, and running the emergency response and information network. Just six months after a previous magnitude 7.1 quake, this earthquake hit on a shallow fault line close to the city and caused much more devastation. Buildings and brick walls collapsed, crushing busses, people, and cars, while rock cliffs and boulders tumbled down hills.

Sara's goal was to help get critical information out to the public and to organizations that needed it. She was part of a management team who oversaw 20 to 30 staff members, ran community meetings, and created a comprehensive international media response. She also helped run the social media and marketing teams as well as the community relations/outreach group that worked with refugees and immigrants. After working through many unnerving aftershocks, Sara had sheet cakes, which her team called "quake cakes," brought into the operation center to help the crew survive the stress.

Sara then took on a temporary position of research social scientist for GNS Science on behalf of the GeoNet project in New Zealand. She had once been the public information coordinator in Christchurch, and her main job was to prepare citizens for possible disasters. After the damage and loss of life from the second quake in 2011, Sara doubted the job she'd done preparing her town, as people didn't feel like they had enough information to know how to stay safe.

At the same time, Sara struggled with her new job at GeoNet and began to question if she could make it as a research scientist. Sara knew she needed more experience and expertise, more tools to help her unpack the science. It was difficult for Sara to admit that she didn't know how to do the job even though she'd had such a long and successful career. She'd been taught that as a woman, she'd have to be "twice as fast and twice as good as a man," and publicly failing was terrifying to her. Her mentor and supervisor, David Johnston, helped her realize she needed to go back to school. He'd already filled out her graduate application and was just waiting for her to ask.

To earn her doctoral degree in English and media studies and communication at Massey University of New Zealand, Sara's goal was to explore how communication specialists and emergency managers developed better ways of teaching communities to be prepared. Doing research was painful and took a lot of patience. The process was slow, and Sara learned that answers don't come easily. Yet her when supervisors advised her to shift her focus to research, Sara couldn't believe she'd conquered one of her biggest obstacles.

While continuing in her social science role as the GeoNet project's information manager, a magnitude 7.8 earthquake rocked Kaikoura, New Zealand, in 2016. This quake tore across 22 different fault lines, setting a world record, and shook for two and half minutes. It rattled people out of their beds, swept railways out to sea, demolished houses, and triggered massive landslides. On call, Sara's phone rang at midnight. She wishes she had stayed calm and collected, but instead found herself running around looking for her pants! She barely remembers getting dressed. Sara tweeted all night, trying to give people the vital information they needed to stay safe and provide scientists with important data to rapidly assess the quake. For eight days, Sara slept under her desk at work or in a hotel room, and she wore the same clothes for four days. She worked like that for four months without a day off, and had lots of quake cake. Today, when Sara returns home after an emergency response, she gives herself crash days to detox from the trauma of the job by surrounding herself with great food (lots of chocolate) and romance or horror movies she's seen before, like the *Evil Dead* films.

Her aunt asked her once why she does this for a living. Time and time again, she sees strangers pulling others out of buildings, opening their homes and feeding people, and donating items and money to help those in need. "Disasters give me hope," Sara told her.

Sara's innovations helped her earn the great honor of being selected for the prestigious two-year, postdoctoral Mendenhall Research Fellowship with the USGS, which encourages researchers to build on their science research and practical skills. So, she and her husband headed back to the United States in 2017, where they felt a bit of reverse culture shock.

Over time, Sara has learned to trust herself more and know when to push through things or shift direction. She was surprised to win the Mendenhall Fellowship because she hadn't followed the traditional path of a research scientist. But that's why they wanted her—because she saw the world differently.

Today, Sara helps coordinate the social sciences program for the US ShakeAlert system at the USGS, publishes 8 or 9 articles a year, runs 15 projects, and works with 20 university researchers in the United States, plus has colleagues around the world. Her role is to figure out how people behave in disasters and use this knowledge to improve the emergency response system. She creates clear messages that help citizens act appropriately with just a few seconds of warning.

When Disasters Collide

The magnitude 6.4 quake that rocked Puerto Rico in 2020 killed one person and devastated the island's southwest coast. It left almost one million without power and hundreds of thousands with no water. As the USGS chief of operations, Sara worked with Federal Emergency Management Agency (FEMA) officials to determine aftershocks forecasts and create messages that could reach through language and cultural barriers. In the offices of the new Freedom Tower in New York City, she briefed the head of FEMA Region 2, Thomas Von Essen, the previous commissioner for the New York City Fire Department during 9/11. Sara learned so much from this powerful and humbling person, and she is inspired by the brave, loyal, and resilient heroes she meets in emergency response work.

Over her long and successful career, Sara has witnessed far too much gender bias and discrimination—especially those forced to change because they are too feminine or don't fit the traditionally masculine norm for science. Many in previous generations have had to conform to this limiting standard, but today, she says women are in a space where they can say, "This is who I am." She recalls being paired with a male mentor who was in his 70s. He told her how he remembered when women were secretaries and remarked that today women are now scientists, just like men. This implied that only men could be scientists and that women were intruders in that masculine space. This was despite the fact that it was a woman—Marie Tharp—who created the first map of the floor of the Atlantic Ocean, which led to the acceptance of the theory of plate tectonics.

Underwater Discovery: The "Backbone of the Earth"

Sixty years ago, women were not encouraged, or sometimes allowed, to study math or science in many colleges.

Marie Tharp, an American geologist and oceanographic cartographer, earned a master's degree from the University of Michigan's petroleum geology program at the Ann Arbor campus during World War II, when women in the country were needed to fill jobs held by men who were off fighting in the war.

In 1957, Marie and her colleague, Bruce Heezen, created the first map of the Atlantic floor, proving that the seafloor was covered in all sorts of geological features and was not flat, like scientists believed. They documented canyons and ridges, and eventually showed a series of mountain ranges that spanned 40,000 miles—the backbone of the earth!

Marie's findings were often undervalued because she was a woman, but she played a direct role in the understanding of plate tectonics.

Opportunities and attitudes are improving, Sara says, but she can recount one too many times when men have degraded the value of women in the sciences. Just 15 years ago, she had engineers tell her, "We're not going to listen to you because of who you are." Sara believes there is still a long way to go. However, there are opportunities available for women in the sciences, and Sara advises women to keep trying until a door opens. She is especially compelled to support trans women and nonbinary people in science because they have an even higher hill to climb. Science should be a safe space for all genders.

Full of wisdom and heart, Sara strives to use research, and her deep connection to the human experience, to help people feel empowered during big natural disasters that often leave us feeling powerless. Not afraid to stand up for justice, she's a fierce protector of women and vulnerable people, and she'll do whatever it takes to figure out ways to communicate with them so they can be safer. "Sometimes, all I can do is witness," she says, "hold their hands, and say, 'I will tell your stories to others.'"

Sara's Top Three Tips for Earthquake Safety

Practice earthquake drills wherever you can to build up mental frameworks for what to do during intense shaking.

Prepare yourself mentally about coming to terms as to what an earthquake might mean for you.

Aftershocks can continue for months after a big earthquake. Prepare for what you will need to do a week, a month, or six months out.

Follow Sara McBride Online:

Twitter: @disastrouscomms

15

Jenny Nakai:
The Justice of Science

Geophysicist Dr. Jenny Nakai uses her voice and scientific knowledge to speak out for others. Her parents taught her that a career should be useful, and Jenny knew she wanted to solve problems. Today, this accomplished scientist uses both her bachelor's degree in mining engineering and postdoctoral degree in geophysics to benefit society. She not only helps to educate the public and the Navajo community about earthquakes and environmental issues but also encourages others to reach for opportunities and break gender, racial, and cultural barriers so that they, too, can make a difference in their own communities. Jenny recently became an operational seismologist with the US Geological Survey Alaska Volcano Observatory, where she gathers and records signals from seismic stations and reviews this data for analysis of volcanic activity. At the observatory, Jenny tests and modifies software and conducts seismic studies related to volcano monitoring in the Aleutian Islands and analyzes seismic data using earthquake location software to detect and locate quakes in Antarctica.

As a child, Jenny lived in different places around the world—from American Samoa, where she learned to swim in the ocean, to the Navajo Reservation, where she got used to moving between Navajo culture and American culture. She loved to read, spend time outside, and attend large family get-togethers when living on the reservation. Jenny's parents made sure they raised an independent thinker and taught her to question everything, which has helped her develop into a spontaneous, compassionate, hard-working person willing to try new things and take risks.

With this insight and knowledge, Jenny has focused her research on resource and environmental challenges in order to evaluate hazards for nearby communities across the Southwest. By studying clusters of earthquakes in the Raton Basin, which is between northern New Mexico and southern Colorado, she hopes to reveal how human actions, like wastewater injection from fracking, cause quakes. She's also studied earthquakes along the Rio Grande Rift, tectonic boundaries in Colorado and New Mexico, in order to help evaluate seismic hazards.

Across the globe, from Alaska to New Zealand, Jenny has been part of research teams using ocean-bottom seismometers and land station data to better understand the causes of tsunami-generating earthquakes, which are a result of the pressure released by tectonic plates that have been locked together over long periods of time. By helping to reveal these mysteries, Jenny aims to find a solution to these killer and silent quakes and tsunamis. During a month in Nepal, Jenny helped install seismometers after the 2015 magnitude 7.8 quake that resulted in 9,000 deaths. She witnessed much sadness and loss of life. Through experiences like this, Jenny is reminded that humans are not in control, especially of the natural world. Yet she finds beauty in people, which motivates her to fight harder to help them.

Jenny has carved out a career in science that also allows her to spread cultural awareness and to mentor Native students back home in the United States. On the reservation, she uses her expertise to fight environmental crises, and organizes workshops that teach students to express themselves and identify with their culture. The goal of this outreach is to find solutions that will change systemic problems that lead to cultural, gender, and racial bias and discrimination in academics and science. Jenny says the work is difficult, but she will never stop trying to find answers to help people, protect the land, and bring equity and respect to all.

Living around the world provided Jenny with a rich childhood. Her mom was a family nurse practitioner with the Indian Health Service. The family moved to American Samoa first so her mom could work with the Indigenous community there. Later, they lived in Texas where her mother earned a master's degree. Jenny really enjoyed the big city life in Texas, but her family mainly lived on and off the Navajo Reservation in Arizona and New Mexico for many years.

Jenny maneuvered between these worlds with ease and learned to become comfortable in both cultures. Her aunt, a middle-school teacher, would send Jenny and her sister boxes of old books from her classroom. Jenny read everything, and books became her friends. But her father encouraged her to get outside too, where she chopped wood, searched for rocks, dug holes for fenceposts, and pulled weeds. She camped, hiked, took road trips with her family, and loved spending time with her aunt, uncle, and grandmother, her Nálí. Jenny remembers sitting with her grandmother for hours while she weaved and spun wool.

Jenny was a shy kid, and changing schools so often was tough. However, growing up around a diverse group of people from many cultures helped her "more than anything in her life." In high school, Jenny didn't like math, yet by college she really enjoyed it, which taught her a good lesson: know how to solve problems. This understanding helped her form her path in science, because for engineers, solving mathematical problems is vital.

Some of Jenny's teachers were discouraging because she was strong-willed. Others appreciated her individuality and spirit, pushing and supporting her. She remembers those who "had compassion . . . and were kind; maybe more kind than they had reason to be." For Jenny, they were the ones who made a difference in her life, inspiring her to do the same for others. Jenny applied for college, figured out her career path in science, and decided on her future—all on her own. On the reservation, education was emphasized, and students were encouraged to come home from school with what they'd learned as a way to contribute "something really good for your people." Jenny wanted to bring her knowledge back.

Over the years, Jenny has lived and breathed earthquakes, and vividly remembers her first. While studying abroad for a semester as an undergraduate in 2007 in Lima, Peru, she was living on the third floor of a house with a local family when a massive magnitude 8.0 quake hit offshore. She recalls the room she was in shaking but did not realize it was a quake. She just stood under the doorframe until the shaking stopped, which seemed endless. Her university organized a relief effort for citizens living close to the epicenter, and Jenny joined, going to the town of Ica, south of Lima—one of two cities hit the hardest. More than 500 people were killed in Peru. Many buildings were destroyed and landslides closed roads. The tsunami had waves over 30 feet high.

For her doctoral program, she spent six weeks in New Zealand as a part of a team working on a ship installing ocean-bottom seismometers that measured the way waves move outward from an earthquake source. She proved not to be the finest example of a sea-fairing scientist, as seasickness plagued her. But she forged through and helped adjust positions of seismometers on the ocean floor and sorted data, all in hopes of learning more about the hazards from megathrust quakes.

Silent Earthquakes

Silent earthquakes, or slow-slip events, are common in New Zealand and can be some of the deadliest natural disasters in the world. They have a deep tremor and a slow slip, which can make them much more dangerous. Global Positioning System (GPS) stations on land help earthquake scientists detect these events through tiny movements or signals. Silent quakes occur when tectonic stress is being relieved from two plates that have been stuck together for a long time. Scientists believe that by studying the slow-slip quake data, they may better understand potential and dangerous megathrust earthquakes and tsunamis that may occur in these areas.

Working with other stellar scientists such as Marianne Karplus, Jenny traveled to Nepal after the 2015 deadly magnitude 7.8 quake, where almost 9,000 died and over 20,000 were hurt. The deadliest quake this region had experienced in over 80 years, it wiped out more than 600,000 homes and damaged an additional 288,000. Deployed to install seismometers shortly after the quake, Jenny witnessed the country still rattled by aftershocks. While working in a town in the high mountains, she recalls how the residents had moved from the hillsides to the valleys due to potential rockfalls or landslides. As aftershocks continued, more large rocks fell and nearly blocked a road they'd just driven on a few hours earlier. With damage to the infrastructure and massive loss of life, Jenny was reminded again of the power of nature over humans. Yet the resilience of the Nepalese people she met, who were warm, welcoming, and strong, made a substantial impact on her. She felt at home among them as their customs were similar to Navajo mannerisms and culture.

Working for the Environmental Protection Agency for the Navajo tribal government for two years, Jenny was exposed to many of the long-lasting environmental issues affecting the reservation. In the 1950 and '60s, many energy companies signed leases to use the tribe's land. But the tribe didn't have anyone help them understand the negative impact of extracting resources, such as oil, natural gas, and uranium, leaving the Navajo with deadly environmental and health concerns that have affected them for generations. Jenny used her expertise to speak out for the community and inform others in hopes of making these companies accountable in a responsible and ethical way.

She performed inspections on major air pollution sources, like natural gas pipeline plants, oil producers, and coal companies, while investigating community complaints of air pollution sources. Like an attorney, she wrote permits, which required learning federal regulations. She also worked with local Navajo communities to inform them of permit changes, and she did other outreach at science fairs and the local community college.

Jenny feels it is important to have the perspective of someone from the reservation to be able to understand these issues from the tribe's point of view. She tries to find ways for tribal members to receive technical expertise, so they can return to their community empowered and in a better position to impact air and water quality and its regulation. She wants to communicate what she knows—no matter how complicated. Education is key to making these changes and saving lives, Jenny says, and she believes there is a way to talk to everybody.

Uranium Mining on the Navajo Reservation

For 40 years, mining companies blasted 4 million tons of uranium from Navajo land to make atomic weapons. Despite low pay and exposure to deadly radiation, many Navajo men worked in the uranium mines on Navajo land during the 1950s boom. The isolated Navajo communities had no idea their men and land were being poisoned, and in the years since, many continue to die from kidney failure or cancer. One study claims that out of 150 Navajo men that worked in a New Mexico uranium mine until 1970, 133 had died of cancer by 1980.

Once the Cold War ended, companies abandoned over 500 mines, leaving thousands of unsealed tunnels, pits, and piles of toxic waste and pools of water close the Navajo community. Cancer rates doubled from the 1970s to the 1990s, and one recent study from the Southwest Research Information Center in conjunction with the federal Centers for Disease Control and Prevention suggests that 27 percent of the participants had high levels of uranium in their urine.

The Environmental Protection Agency has removed some of the toxic waste and rebuilt a portion of the homes in these areas. Several mining corporations have compensated the Navajo for cleanup. This inequity is systemic of the bigger problems that continue to affect low-income communities of color, and why people like Jenny Nakai use scientific expertise to bring about justice.

Jenny wants to open a path forward for Native Americans. By organizing workshops, she creates spaces for students to express their identity and culture but also teach confidence-building and risk-taking. As a part of program called Girls on Rocks, Jenny takes 16-year-old girls into the wilderness to learn about nature and science. She also helps organize scientific conferences that will increase leadership awareness of underrepresented minority issues.

Jenny is currently working on assisting Native students and other minorities in their transition to college and graduate school, trying to change the insidious systemic problems that exist in professional organizations, academia, and the scientific field in general. She spends a lot of time trying to get people to listen to what she has to say about bias and discrimination, which can be more difficult than getting her research published! Jenny says that when she sees Native students she has helped, who are now confident, ambitious, and compassionate, she is very happy.

For Jenny, life is often about fighting against deep-rooted barriers. Nobody ever tells her flat out that they are discriminating against her because she is female or Native American. Accounts of racism and prejudice are rarely that overt. In high school, she was encouraged to study humanities and writing instead of STEM-related fields, despite her interest. As an undergraduate in college, she didn't have the advanced math classes she needed to major in engineering and found little support or encouragement. So she did it on her own, taking both precalculus and trigonometry in the summer so she could take calculus with the rest of the engineering majors.

Jenny has constantly had to overcome other people's low expectations and prejudices, which has made her journey a lot longer and a lot more tiresome. Along the way, she's been frustrated by narrow-mindedness, stereotypes, and the assumption that she hasn't done her own work or that she grew up poor. But Jenny does not relent easily. "I am always fighting," she says, and admits that it gets tiring.

In her field, Jenny has battled those who tell her to "play nice" and "keep my mouth shut" because she's lucky to be in the room. She encourages both women and other misrepresented groups to resist the pressure to conform. Do what you know is right based on your own background and values, she says, and question everything. This may make life more difficult, but living this way, she finds peace and likes who she is.

Family has carried Jenny through the good and bad times. She is especially inspired by her Aunt Bessie, her father's sister, who was a traditional Navajo through and through. Her aunt only spoke Navajo and lived in a remote section of the reservation. Jenny remembers how rich her life was, caring for 60 sheep and other livestock, raising her own kids and grandkids, and weaving in the Navajo tradition. She was kind to everyone, even those who did not wish her well. Jenny feels lucky to have had her aunt, a woman who lived in harmony with everything around her and who was humble, understated, funny, and incredibly tough—mentally and physically. Aunt Bessie taught her to be a reasonable human being and, through example, showed Jenny Navajo philosophy and how to live life in the best way.

Committed to her career and giving back to her community, Jenny only has a few spare moments each day. She enjoys mountain adventures and traveling—especially the drama, harshness, and wildness of the landscape in places like Tibet. She likes to explore and wants to experience new places and ways of living. Being on her own during these trips gets her "out of her head." Jenny takes long runs in the mountains. One of her favorite runs in Norway ended up being 14 hours of climbing up and down mountains, crossing valleys, and getting lost, hungry, and emotional. Jenny says it was one of the best days she's ever had.

This spontaneous, dedicated, and talented scientist believes that the world has more to offer than what is in the imagination. She doesn't really have any end goals in life and takes things as they come, but in the future she would love to have a small vegetable garden and to live in the mountains or near the ocean. Jenny reflects on the tough times when she was spiraling, yet she never doubts her own determination. Her resilience and compassion motivate her to keep moving toward change. To keep looking under the earth. To keep encouraging and fighting for equity for Diné, the Navajo people.

Jenny's Top Three Tips for Earthquake Safety

Drop, cover, and hold on!

Store lots of water. FEMA says to store at least one gallon, per person, per day, and consider a two-week supply for each member in your family.

Learn more about what is happening during an earthquake—such as how to understand seismic waves, or P and S waves.

P, or primary or pressure waves, arrive first during a quake and can travel through solids and liquids. They shake in the direction they are moving. Dogs can feel them before the earthquake hits the crust of the planet.

S, or secondary or shear waves, come after. They are much slower and can only travel through solids. They shake vertically and horizontally and cause more damage.

Follow Jenny Nakai Online:

YouTube: www.youtube.com/watch?v=fYcPn7xtd_s and
www.youtube.com/watch?v=pognAJUB2UY

Afterword
Find Your Passion

Many of the women in this book had no idea they would end up scientists studying how the processes of the earth can lead to earthquakes, tsunamis, or volcanic eruptions. As girls, some of them hated math, whether it was due to a learning disability or discouragement from a teacher. Others were never ushered into science as a kid. They might have been curious about the world, but due to traditional social expectations, or gender or racial bias, they didn't have role models or mentors to look up to.

Maybe their path into earthquake science was a total coincidence. They might have started out in different careers or majors, and because of an earthquake, their plans were shaken up, topsy-turvy, like social scientist Kate Gonzalez Long or geologist Dr. Wendy Bohon. Suddenly, they wanted to help fix things that were broken. Or help people through struggles, like Dr. Jenny Nakai. Maybe, with encouragement from their family and friends, like Dr. Annemarie Baltay Sundstrom or Carolina Rojas, these women wanted to be adventurous and take risks. Or just see deeper through advanced technology like Dr. Clara Yoon. See farther and wider within the earth, like Dr. Peggy Hellweg and Dr. Susan Hough. Uncover mysteries from under the ocean, like Dr. Valerie Sahakian or Dr. Lori Dengler. And peer into deadly volcanoes, like Debbie Weiser or Beth Bartel.

You see where this is going, right?

Life doesn't always go as planned. Often, the path you think you're on leads somewhere totally unexpected. Yet whatever path you choose, make sure it belongs to you. Don't be afraid to try new things. Carve out your road and mix it up. Many of these women took nontraditional paths into science or communications or combined different interests and passions to create a whole new place for themselves in their fields. And, you've heard it before, but they all expected to fail throughout their career. They learned to grow from it, and to be excited about the surprises and unexpected things that come with it.

So keep your eyes open. Find what makes your heart skip, and then do your research. It might be science. Or math. Maybe you love words. Animals. Dance. History. Coding. The sky's the limit. It's up to you.

Your passion.

Your dreams.

Your life.

Time to get living.

Acknowledgments

Writing *Quake Chasers* connected me to a group of amazing human beings. These brilliant, compassionate, creative, funny, adventurous, and progressive-thinking women inspire me. These quake chasers give me hope that, along with their big hearts and passion to prepare, protect, and educate, science can and will prevail. I can't thank them enough for reminding me of the power we have to make change in this world if we collaborate, innovate, and dedicate ourselves to collectively gearing our planet in the right direction. For that, I am forever thankful.

I am lucky enough to have a family that never doubts my own passion to write, especially on those long, crazy late-night-walking-on-the-treadmill writing sessions. I cannot thank my phenomenal partner in life, my husband Dan, and my own two creative and adventurous kids, Grayson and Nova, enough. They rally around me and keep me afloat—plus my two office rescue pups, Ollie and Addie, that never left my side during lockdown as I wrote this book. And to my amazing brother and dad—wow! I will never take your love for granted. I have the best human-animal squad in the whole world.

To my wonderful agent, Ann Leslie Tuttle, for her never-ending support and validation, which means more than she'll ever know. And my editor, Jerome Pohlen, for his guidance and for giving me the opportunity to weave *Quake Chasers* into this incredible Women in Power series, which I hope inspires and helps people prepare for the shaking below our feet. To my writing tribe: thank you for allowing me to stand on your shoulders, and reminding me to never give up on my dreams.

Lastly, I want to express my gratitude to all the women in my life—starting with my own mom, who never quite had the chance to be who she wanted to be. I saw you, and miss you terribly. You bestowed your creative and compassionate gifts onto me, and I am eternally thankful. From all my incredible teachers—Mrs. Fielder (fourth grade) and Ms. Pfeffer (fifth grade) to Professor Susan Paterno (California State University, Long Beach)—who empowered me, reminding me that I had the courage and talent to be a writer even when I didn't believe it myself. To my second mom, Eleanor St. Clair, who always opened the door to the possibilities and showed me how to fully engage in life. Marilyn Gould—my mentor, friend, and first real writing teacher—you will always inspire me, and make me laugh and cry with your stories.

And to my sisters—you know who you are—thank you for always encircling me in love and laughter.

And to my students, find the thing that makes your heart race. Dive in and use that passion to take care of this world and make it more equitable, more compassionate, and more beautiful.

Notes

1: Annemarie Baltay Sundstrom

"do something important": All quotes from original author interview with Annemarie Baltay Sundstrom on February 22, 2021, or a follow-up e-mail response.

2: Wendy Bohon

"reason she became a scientist": All quotes from original author interview with Wendy Bohon on February 17, 2021, and March 2, 2021, unless otherwise noted here.

"These explorer Barbies": Nalini Nadkarni, "She Helped Mattel Create New Line of Scientist Barbies." *Philadelphia Inquirer*, February 1, 2020, accessed April 15, 2022, www.inquirer. com/life/scientist-barbie-inspired-by-woman-ecologist -20200201.html.

3: Peggy Hellweg

"walking encyclopedia": All quotes from original author interview with Peggy Hellweg on December 6 and 18, 2019.

4: Debbie Weiser

"nerdy love": All quotes from original author interview with Debbie Weiser on February 28, 2020, and March 23, 2021.

5: Clara Yoon

"equally scary and fascinating": All quotes from original author interview with Clara Yoon through e-mail on March 10 and 19, 2021.

6: Lori Dengler

"ask questions and listen": All quotes from original author interview with Lori Dengler on November 2, 2019, unless otherwise noted here.

"fess up" and *"out-of-the-box thinkers"*: Lori Dengler, "The Whiteness Problem in Earth Sciences," *Times Standard*, June 28, 2020, www.times-standard.com/2020/06/21/lori -dengler-the-whiteness-problem-in-earth-sciences/.

7: Susan Hough

"long leash": All quotes from original author interview with Susan Hough on October 18, 2019, and April 28, 2020, or a follow-up e-mail response on April 30.

Mercalli Intensity Scale: US Geological Survey, "The Modified Mercalli Intensity Scale, USGS, https://www.usgs.gov /natural-hazards/earthquake-hazards/science/modified -mercalli-intensity-scale?qt-science_center objects=0#qt -science_center_objects.

8: Marianne Karplus

"Had their stuff": All quotes from original author interview with Marianne Karplus on February 18 and 28, 2021.

9: Edith Carolina Rojas

"fighters, not quiet": All quotes from original author interview with Edith Rojas on October 18 and 26, 2019, or follow-up text messages in October 2019.

10: Valerie Sahakian

"weren't for girls": All quotes from original author interview with Valerie Sahakian on March 11 and 24, 2020.

11: Beth Bartel

"middle-of-nowhere": All quotes from original author interview with Beth Bartel on March 2, 2020, or a follow-up e-mail response April 9, 2020.

12: Donyelle Davis

"sometimes you have": All quotes from original author interview with Donyelle Davis through e-mail on April 20 and 21, 2020.

13: Kate Gonzalez Long

"everyone got that manual": All quotes from original author interview with Kate Gonzalez Long on February 27, 2020, and March 1, 2020.

14: Sara McBride

"determine her": All quotes from original author interview with
Sara McBride on March 5, 2020, and April 19, 2020.

15: Jenny Nakai

"more than anything": All quotes from original author interview with Jenny Nakai through e-mail on February 28,
2020.